EGYPT: CHALLENGES AND OPPORTUNITIES FOR U.S. POLICY

HEARING

BEFORE THE

SUBCOMMITTEE ON
THE MIDDLE EAST AND NORTH AFRICA

OF THE

COMMITTEE ON FOREIGN AFFAIRS
HOUSE OF REPRESENTATIVES

ONE HUNDRED FOURTEENTH CONGRESS

SECOND SESSION

JUNE 15, 2016

Serial No. 114–194

Printed for the use of the Committee on Foreign Affairs

Available via the World Wide Web: http://www.foreignaffairs.house.gov/ or
http://www.gpo.gov/fdsys/

U.S. GOVERNMENT PUBLISHING OFFICE

20–455PDF   WASHINGTON : 2016

For sale by the Superintendent of Documents, U.S. Government Publishing Office
Internet: bookstore.gpo.gov   Phone: toll free (866) 512–1800; DC area (202) 512–1800
Fax: (202) 512–2104   Mail: Stop IDCC, Washington, DC 20402–0001

COMMITTEE ON FOREIGN AFFAIRS

EDWARD R. ROYCE, California, *Chairman*

CHRISTOPHER H. SMITH, New Jersey
ILEANA ROS-LEHTINEN, Florida
DANA ROHRABACHER, California
STEVE CHABOT, Ohio
JOE WILSON, South Carolina
MICHAEL T. McCAUL, Texas
TED POE, Texas
MATT SALMON, Arizona
DARRELL E. ISSA, California
TOM MARINO, Pennsylvania
JEFF DUNCAN, South Carolina
MO BROOKS, Alabama
PAUL COOK, California
RANDY K. WEBER SR., Texas
SCOTT PERRY, Pennsylvania
RON DeSANTIS, Florida
MARK MEADOWS, North Carolina
TED S. YOHO, Florida
CURT CLAWSON, Florida
SCOTT DesJARLAIS, Tennessee
REID J. RIBBLE, Wisconsin
DAVID A. TROTT, Michigan
LEE M. ZELDIN, New York
DANIEL DONOVAN, New York

ELIOT L. ENGEL, New York
BRAD SHERMAN, California
GREGORY W. MEEKS, New York
ALBIO SIRES, New Jersey
GERALD E. CONNOLLY, Virginia
THEODORE E. DEUTCH, Florida
BRIAN HIGGINS, New York
KAREN BASS, California
WILLIAM KEATING, Massachusetts
DAVID CICILLINE, Rhode Island
ALAN GRAYSON, Florida
AMI BERA, California
ALAN S. LOWENTHAL, California
GRACE MENG, New York
LOIS FRANKEL, Florida
TULSI GABBARD, Hawaii
JOAQUIN CASTRO, Texas
ROBIN L. KELLY, Illinois
BRENDAN F. BOYLE, Pennsylvania

AMY PORTER, *Chief of Staff*   THOMAS SHEEHY, *Staff Director*
JASON STEINBAUM, *Democratic Staff Director*

————

SUBCOMMITTEE ON THE MIDDLE EAST AND NORTH AFRICA

ILEANA ROS-LEHTINEN, Florida, *Chairman*

STEVE CHABOT, Ohio
JOE WILSON, South Carolina
DARRELL E. ISSA, California
RANDY K. WEBER SR., Texas
RON DeSANTIS, Florida
MARK MEADOWS, North Carolina
TED S. YOHO, Florida
CURT CLAWSON, Florida
DAVID A. TROTT, Michigan
LEE M. ZELDIN, New York

THEODORE E. DEUTCH, Florida
GERALD E. CONNOLLY, Virginia
BRIAN HIGGINS, New York
DAVID CICILLINE, Rhode Island
ALAN GRAYSON, Florida
GRACE MENG, New York
LOIS FRANKEL, Florida
BRENDAN F. BOYLE, Pennsylvania

CONTENTS

EGYPT: CHALLENGES AND OPPORTUNITIES FOR U.S. POLICY

WEDNESDAY, JUNE 15, 2016

HOUSE OF REPRESENTATIVES,
SUBCOMMITTEE ON THE MIDDLE EAST AND NORTH AFRICA,
COMMITTEE ON FOREIGN AFFAIRS,
Washington, DC.

The committee met, pursuant to notice, at 10:03 a.m., in room 2172, Rayburn House Office Building, Hon. Ileana Ros-Lehtinen (chairman of the subcommittee) presiding.

Ms. ROS-LEHTINEN. The subcommittee will come to order.

After recognizing myself and Mr. Deutch, the ranking member, for 5 minutes each for our opening statements, I will then recognize other members seeking recognition for 1 minute. We will then hear from our witnesses. And you will notice an empty seat, but she is coming right over, getting through security.

Without objection, the witnesses' prepared statements will be made a part of the record. Members may have 5 days to insert statements and questions for the record subject to the length limitation in the rules.

And the Chair now recognizes herself for 5 minutes.

This is the third hearing of our subcommittee that we have had on Egypt in a little over a year, demonstrating the importance of and our subcommittee's commitment to Egypt's role in a volatile region, as well as the concern of our members that they have on current U.S. policy toward our ally.

The political, economic, and security challenges that Egypt is facing right now, they are numerous, they are interdependent. It is extremely difficult, for example, for President Sisi to make necessary structural reforms to Egypt's economy without potentially undermining the fragile political support he is leaning on to bring much-needed stability to the country.

Conversely, if these economic reforms are not made soon, we may see a return of the unrest that we saw on Egyptian streets not too long ago. And it is in this context that Egypt is facing growing security threats from an expanding ISIS and its Sinai Province affiliate, from al-Qaeda-linked groups, from militias, from extremists in Libya, and from particularly violent factions of the Muslim Brotherhood. Sinai Province has formed terrorist cells that are targeting both Egyptian and Israeli military personnel and civilians, and has already killed hundreds of Egyptian soldiers is continuing to target the peacekeeping operations or the MFO, Multinational Force of

(1)

Observers in the Sinai, prompting the Pentagon to reposition U.S. troops and reconsider its presence there.

There is more and more evidence that ISIS is attempting to link its operations in the Sinai and eastern Egypt to its presence in the Western Desert that sits along the extremely porous border with Libya. And there are growing reports of increased activity in southern Egypt and the Nile Valley, including in greater Cairo, which has seen IEDs and shootings like the one that claimed the lives of eight Egyptian policemen last month.

While Egypt has been trying to keep up with these threats, it is increasingly clear that Egypt must also adopt a counterinsurgency approach that will allow it to get a handle on the problem before it gets worse.

While the security situation remains a high priority, I am extremely concerned by the government's attitude toward human rights, its crackdowns on civil society, its quashing of dissent. I was disappointed to see that the government froze the assets of yet another NGO just yesterday as part of an ongoing case which began in 2011 and targeted U.S. NGOs like IRI, whose president joins us here today.

Forty-three NGO workers in this case were unjustly convicted in 2013, as we all remember, and I continue to call on President Sisi to do everything in his power, including working with the Egyptian Parliament and with the judicial system to find a way to pardon these workers as soon as possible. The government needs to find a way to open up civil society and allow Egyptians to participate and thrive in public life or risk exacerbating the very problems it is trying to avoid.

In Egypt, the economy is perhaps the biggest challenge of all. Infusions of cash from the Gulf States, especially from Saudi Arabia, as well as loans from the World Bank, the IMF, and others, have managed to keep the economy afloat for the time being. But these investments aren't likely to stimulate growth in the long term, and the government has to make difficult structural reforms like reducing the bloated public payroll and passing the long-promised value-added tax. Unemployment, especially among youth, remains high, and around 60 percent of the population is poor and living on subsidies.

One bright spot on the economy horizon has been the Egyptian-American Enterprise Fund, which Congress authorized in 2012 and has been successfully investing in Egypt's private sector to create jobs and support sustainable development.

The Enterprise Fund, as with all the aid that Congress has appropriated, is an example of how much the United States wants to help Egypt as both an ally and a strong supporter of peace in that troubled region. But the Egyptian Government also needs to help us help them, and that includes allowing our Economic Support Funds, or ESF monies, to be programmed. As of March 31, there is a backlog of approximately $900 million in ESF for Egypt because the government has held up permits for our implementing partners on everything from democracy and governance to education and health care.

That is why I was happy to sign a letter this month, alongside Chairman Royce, Ranking Member Engel, and the co-chairs of the

Tunisia Caucus, asking the Secretary of State to reprogram up to $20 million of this money for Tunisia. This is not meant to be a slight against Egypt, but it makes little sense to continue letting these funds sit in the pipeline when they can be spent somewhere else. Someplace like Tunisia, which is in desperate need of the funds and is willing to let us help.

Egypt is an important strategic ally that is struggling on a number of fronts, and as we discuss the challenges and opportunities for U.S. policy here today, I continue to believe that the best way to help is through encouragement and assistance as a friend.

And with that, I am pleased to yield to the ranking member, Mr. Deutch of Florida.

Mr. DEUTCH. Thank you. Thank you, Madam Chairman, and thanks for our witnesses for appearing today.

First, I want to thank you, Madam Chairman, and Mr. Connolly for commissioning a series of GAO reports on our assistance to Egypt. The most recent report issued in April highlighted some of the serious challenges faced by Department of Defense and the Department of State in securing compliance from the Egyptian Government on end-use monitoring of our assistance. And I find this troubling. When we work together in partnership with the government, that government should not be hindering our ability to ensure that our assistance is going to where it is meant to go and doing what it is meant to do.

Second, I want to unequivocally state that I value the U.S.-Egypt relationship. I value Egypt's role in the region. I want to see the Egyptian people prosper. And I particularly want to thank the Egyptian Foreign Ministry for the condolences it sent to the victims of the horrific terror attack in the chairman and my home State just days ago.

But it is becoming increasingly difficult to discuss the U.S.-Egypt relationship outside its security context, and so while I have supported and I continue to support the Sisi government and the President's commitment to fighting terror and keeping peace in the region, I am quite troubled by the direction of the country when it comes to civil society and human rights. I do understand that it can be challenging to balance security and human rights.

Egypt is coming out of a period of great turmoil. As Egypt's leaders look around the region, they see numerous threats to stability, and there is no doubt that we share our Egyptian partners' commitment to preventing ISIS and its affiliates from dominating Sinai, but I urge our friends not to silence the discourse on human rights. Engage with civil society, democracy, and human right activists. Work together. Have the tough conversations. A lack of inclusive governing will yield greater instability.

One area I am deeply concerned about is the foreign funding of the NGOs' case. Now, this subcommittee has held many hearings on the arrest, trial, and conviction of the 43 NGO employees. Mr. Green, you have been present for several of those hearings. The idea that the government is now going to reopen the NGO trial and add new defendants is deeply disturbing. The only reason this case should be reopened is to pardon each and every one of the 43 individuals. And I want to commend the chair for continued advocacy on behalf of those who were so wrongfully convicted in this case.

President Sisi has been tasked with the difficult job of reviving Egypt's economy after years of mismanagement. I want to commend him for taking seriously recommendations for reform from the World Bank and the IMF. Last year, the economy grew at its fastest rate since 2010. Buoyed by generous financial support from the gulf, Egypt has found some economic relief. But diminished foreign currency reserves are making it increasingly difficult to import fuel and food, and water shortages are beginning to impact rural areas. The government must continue to work with international financial institutions to push ahead with necessary reforms to meet these challenges.

On the security front, Egypt faces dangerous threats from the Sinai. I commend the Egypt military for its commitment to rooting out terrorism and to taking seriously the need to improve government services and infrastructure for the people of Sinai.

I extend condolences to the dozens of Egyptian soldiers and their families who have lost their lives fighting this terrorism, and President Sisi deserves to be commended for speaking out against violent Islamic extremism.

In addition, I want to thank the Egyptian Government for its continued cooperation with Israel in the Sinai and its continuing efforts to prevent Hamas from using tunnels to smuggle dangerous weapons to Gaza.

President Sisi has made clear his interest in brokering peace between Israel and the Palestinians, and both have welcomed his involvement in the process with trust-building on both sides. He can be a strong voice for two states living side by side in peace and security.

Our $1.3 billion of security assistance to Egypt is critical in the fight against ISIS both in the Sinai and in Libya. The fragile political situation in Libya has created space for ISIS to use Libya as a training ground for its fighters. To that end, assisting Egypt in controlling its 1,100 kilometer border with Libya is essential to preventing ISIS fighters from launching cross-border attacks or using Egypt as a transit point to the greater Middle East.

I applaud the administration's recognition of the need to refocus our assistance on counterterrorism. The threats facing Egypt are not countered with tanks and planes alone but with a strong intelligence apparatus and regional and bilateral intelligence-sharing, and we have a real opportunity here to help Egypt confront and root out terrorism.

I want to see the people of Egypt succeed. I want to see the future of Egypt that so many millions poured into the streets demanding. I believe President Sisi wants his country and his people to thrive, but to do so will take real political will to confront terrorism to reform the economy and to give space for civil society to grow and to thrive. These are not easy tasks, nor are they accomplished without the support of the United States.

And I look to our witnesses today to help us better understand how we can be an effective partner for Egypt while continuing to advocate for the basic human rights and values that this country was founded upon. And with that, I yield back.

Ms. ROS-LEHTINEN. Well said. Thank you so much, Mr. Deutch.

I will now recognize members for statements that they would like to make.

Mr. Wilson of South Carolina.

Mr. WILSON OF SOUTH CAROLINA. Thank you, Chairman Ileana Ros-Lehtinen and Ranking Member Deutch, for holding this important hearing.

Over the last decade, Egypt has been faced with political and social instability. Egypt has been and will continue to be a valued ally in an unstable region in support of American interests and worldwide interests in the global war on terrorism. I am grateful my son Julian served with the Army National Guard in Egypt with Operation Bright Star, an indication of U.S.-Egyptian cooperation. And he was impressed by the talented citizens of Egypt.

I believe that we need to continue our military and economic support while we closely monitor whether the money that is being provided is wisely spent. Egypt continues to face a growing threat from Islamic terrorists, most recently, the Egypt Air flight that was destroyed in the eastern Mediterranean Sea to the Metrojet flight that exploded over the Sinai on October 31, killing 209 Russian tourists.

Egypt exists within a very dangerous neighborhood, and it is very critical that we maintain our support, also maintaining our moral responsibilities, promoting IRI as a very positive NGO.

I look forward to hearing from our witnesses regarding how the United States can help ensure that Egypt is back on track to be a success for prosperity for its citizens.

Ms. ROS-LEHTINEN. Thank you very much, and congratulations on your son's military service. It is a long tradition there. Good for you, Joe.

Mr. Connolly of Virginia.

Mr. CONNOLLY. Thank you, Madam Chairman, and thank you for our collaboration on the GAO report our friend Deutch cited.

I think, you know, the relationship with Egypt is a critical relationship. It has got to be one we work out. But American patience is not unlimited, and the Egyptian leverage on the relationship is also not unlimited. There is a desire in this country and a growing desire in this body to hold the current Egyptian Government accountable for human rights violations, accountable for security infringements, accountable for how it treats civil society, especially the NGOs we have worked with.

I met with a lot of those NGOs when I was in Cairo, and I think the Egyptian Government was counting on the United States once the Americans got out of the country to frankly wash their hands of the Egyptian staff and volunteers of these NGOs. That is not the case, and I hope this hearing makes that very clear. And I know Ambassador Green is going to make that point. We stand by those brave young men and women who were trying to make for a better society in their own country, and I know we are going to hear more about that in this hearing. Thank you, Madam Chairman.

Ms. ROS-LEHTINEN. Thank you, Mr. Connolly. Thank you very much.

Thank you, Mr. Rohrabacher. We are pleased to recognize you for any opening statement you might make.

Mr. ROHRABACHER. Thank you very much for holding this hearing, and I appreciate you and the ranking member and the work that you have put into this.

Let me just note that I am a co-chairman with the Egyptian Caucus, and as such I have been to Egypt a number of times in recent days. And let me just state for the record that I believe that President el-Sisi and the democratic people in Egypt who want to have a legitimate democratic government are under attack by forces that would murder them.

So whatever we are doing when we are talking about Egypt, let's understand we are talking about people who are fighting forces that would murder them and create a caliphate that would be allied with terrorists. In fact, if President el-Sisi and his efforts are defeated, you could expect a collapse of resistance to this radical Islamic terrorist movement that threatens the world.

They are at an equivalent of where we were at immediately after Pearl Harbor. The fact is what did we do when we were under attack? Yes, there were things that we would never tolerate in our society today. We put large numbers of American citizens, Japanese-Americans in camps. Yes, that did not indicate what type of government, what type of country we had, but it did indicate that we were at war with an enemy that had murdered our own people and would continue to do so.

That is what is going on in Egypt today. Those people are on the front lines. President el-Sisi and his democratic allies and the moderate Muslim community there are under attack by the very same terrorists that would again create a caliphate and threaten the entire world. We have faced this terrorism here. We have faced it in Orlando. We have faced it in San Bernardino. We have faced it at the Boston Marathon.

This radical Islamic terrorism threat to the world is something that we need to recognize. And we need to recognize that people like President el-Sisi and the good people of Egypt are on the front lines, and we need to back them as much as we can so that we can—because we know if they lose, we lose.

Thank you very much, Madam Chairman.

Ms. ROS-LEHTINEN. Thank you, Mr. Rohrabacher.

Ms. Frankel of Florida.

Ms. FRANKEL. Madam Chair, I thank the witnesses for being here, and I would like to hear what they have to say so I yield back to you.

Ms. ROS-LEHTINEN. Thank you very much, Ms. Frankel.

And, Dr. Yoho of Florida?

Mr. YOHO. No comment.

Ms. ROS-LEHTINEN. Okay. Thank you so much to our witnesses. First, we are pleased to welcome back a great friend of our subcommittee, Ambassador Mark Green, a former colleague of ours. He is the president of the International Republican Institute. He is a former U.S. Ambassador to Tanzania and served as a Member of Congress representing Wisconsin's Eighth District from '97 to 2007. It is always a delight to see you, Mr. Ambassador. I love following you on Twitter.

Next, we welcome Mr.—I am going to try my best—Mokhtar Awad, who is a research fellow in the Program on Extremism at

George Washington University's Center for Cyber and Homeland Security. Prior to this, Mr. Awad worked as a Research Associate at the Center for American Progress. We welcome you to our subcommittee, Mr. Awad.

And lastly, we welcome Ms. Amy Hawthorne, who is the deputy director for research at the Project on Middle East Democracy. Prior to this, Ms. Hawthorne served as a resident senior fellow with the Atlantic Council's Middle East Program where she focused on U.S. policy toward Egypt. We welcome you also, Ms. Hawthorne.

We are pleased to have all of you here today. As I had said, your statements will be made a part of the record, and we will now hear your synthesized version starting with our friend Mark.

STATEMENT OF THE HONORABLE MARK GREEN, PRESIDENT, INTERNATIONAL REPUBLICAN INSTITUTE

Ambassador GREEN. Thank you, Madam Chair, Ranking Member Deutch, and members of the committee. I appreciate the opportunity to testify. And I also want to thank you for the tremendous support that you have shown, that all of you have shown relating to Egypt's indefensible NGO foreign funding trial.

As you know and as has been alluded to, Egypt wrongfully and outrageously convicted 43 innocent staff from IRI, NDI, Freedom House, and others. And I am grateful that you continue to make pardons for these victims your highest priority in discussions with the top Egyptian officials.

One year ago, Madam Chair, I testified on Tunisia's democratic tradition. I offered optimism about the progress it was making and suggested that it deserved additional support. I wish I could be similarly optimistic here today, but sadly, I believe that Egypt is moving on an uncertain and dangerous trajectory.

There is no doubt, as many of you have said, that Egypt remains a very important ally and strategic partner for America's interests in that part of the world, but there is also little doubt, however, that the problems that are in Egypt continue to get worse. Polarization and the threat of extremism are on the rise. President Sisi's counterterrorism campaign is making precious little headway in my opinion while risking even greater alienation of the local population. Instead of forging an effective effort to root out extremists and extremism, I worry that the government's primary response seems to be an even greater crackdown on dissent.

There has been an increase in extrajudicial forced disappearances, over 1,800 reported cases in 2015 alone. Mass trials and collective convictions based on vague charges of harming national interests have become the norm.

Madam Chair, it is my strong belief in IRI's long experience that counterterrorism and military operations alone will never be a sufficient response to genuine real extremist threats that they face. Egypt needs to enlist the help of its civil society, not crush it. It should avoid measures like its 2013 anti-protest law that curtails citizens' ability to participate peacefully in public meetings or its 2015 counterterrorism law that punishes journalists who stray from official government narratives. President Sisi has defended the crackdown on civil society calling it fourth generation warfare, the notion that media and civil society groups that aren't lockstep with the government are somehow waging war against the Egypt State.

Madam Chair, history warns us of the dangers when conspiracy theory becomes official policy. Just ask those 43 wrongly convicted NGO workers who are still unable to travel freely in some parts of the world, and the Egyptian staff who have been cut off from their families over these years. Now, the Egyptian Government appears to be doubling down on its approach. As was mentioned, it has reopened and apparently widened the NGO case with as many as 47 Egyptian and international organizations now being threatened with criminal prosecution.

But despite this bleak picture, IRI and other international organizations still hope that Egypt will one day reclaim its strong civil society and citizen-responsive government traditions. At IRI we continue to work with peaceful democratic Egyptians through programs taking place offshore in third country locations. We still hope to assist civil society and political party reformers to improve governance and to combat the alienation and anger that extremism depends upon. We are proud that, despite the many obvious challenges, a recent independent evaluation of our Egypt programs found promising results and reason for continued engagement.

Madam Chair, I respectfully offer the following recommendations for the subcommittee to consider: First, since Egyptian obstinacy has apparently created a backlog of U.S.-Egypt assistance funds to the tune of $700 million or more, I would urge the U.S. to redirect much of that backlog to places where significant democratic strides are being made, places like Tunisia.

Second, the funds that are going to Egypt I believe a significant portion of that should be used to engage democratic actors and build their skills for a future democratic breakthrough.

And then finally, U.S. administration officials, Members of Congress, and staff at every level should continue to raise the foreign funding case at every opportunity. We should make it clear that reopening the case and expanding it is unconditionally unacceptable. And of course, continue to insist that the only solution to the 2013 verdict is full pardons by President Sisi.

Madam Chair, a recent Economist article suggested that if Egypt does well, it can lift the region, whereas its collapse would represent a threat to the entire Middle East and Europe. I would add the United States to that list as well.

Thank you, Madam Chair.

[The prepared statement of Ambassador Green follows:]

Congressional Testimony

Egypt: Challenges and Opportunities for U.S. Policy

Testimony by Ambassador Mark Green
President
International Republican Institute

U.S. House Committee on Foreign Affairs
Subcommittee on the Middle East and North Africa
June 15, 2016

INTRODUCTION

Chairman Ros-Lehtinen, Ranking Member Deutch, Members of the Committee, thank you for this opportunity to testify on the troubling state of affairs in Egypt. I also want to extend my personal gratitude to Chairman Ros-Lehtinen for the support that you and your staff have shown to the International Republican Institute (IRI) and our peer organizations in the Egyptian government's NGO "foreign funding trial." As you know all too well, the Egyptian government resorted to actions and procedures violating every internationally accepted standard (as well as human decency) to harass, prosecute and wrongfully convict forty-three (43) innocent staff from IRI, the National Democratic Institute (NDI), Freedom House, the International Center for Journalists (ICFJ) and the German Konrad Adenaur Foundation (KAS). Most were given long prison sentences in absentia. This outrage is still unresolved, but we are most appreciative of the steadfast efforts of Members of Congress who continue to raise the matter with top Egyptian officials.

Approximately one year ago, I had the privilege to testify before this committee on the topic of Tunisia's democratic transition. I offered my cautious optimism for the progress Tunisia was making, and suggested it merited additional U.S. support. Madam Chair, I wish I could offer a similarly optimistic opinion today on Egypt but, sadly, the opposite is true. Egypt is on an uncertain and dangerous trajectory. In short, we should all be deeply concerned about the plight of citizen rights and freedoms, the prospects for long term stability and the future of the U.S.-Egypt relationship itself.

U.S. - EGYPT STRATEGIC RELATIONSHIP

Egypt has been a valued strategic partner to the United States for much of the last five decades. It remains a vitally important country in the Middle East and North Africa region given its peace treaty with our ally Israel, control of the Suez Canal, enormous cultural influence and status as the Arab World's most populous country. All of this is reflected in the massive financial support our government provides each year to Egypt and its military. In Fiscal Year 2017, the Administration is requesting approximately $1.3 billion in military aid and an additional $150 million in economic assistance.[1]

In the immediate aftermath of the 2011 revolution that overthrew Hosni Mubarak, elected President Mohammed Morsi and the Muslim Brotherhood were unquestionably leading Egypt in the wrong direction. This destructive course was most evident in how the Brotherhood excluded

---

[1] https://www.fas.org/sgp/crs/midcast/RL33003.pdf

the political opposition, notably minority Christians, when it revamped the Egyptian constitution. Morsi's willingness to employ street violence as a political tactic against secular civil society opponents was further evidence of the Brotherhood's repressive leadership.

Morsi's removal from power through a military coup prevented Egypt from careening down a dangerous path of combative political Islamism. However, we must also acknowledge that in the three years since, Egypt's internal situation has simply not improved under President Abdel Fatah El Sisi; to the contrary, polarization within Egyptian society and the threat of extremism are growing steadily worse both in the Sinai and within Egyptian society.

Economically, Egypt would be in a free fall right now were it not for significant financial aid from several Gulf States, including a recently announced $22 billion oil deal and assistance package from Saudi Arabia.[2] This latest infusion is very unlikely to overcome the economy's significant structural challenges. The situation is compounded by declining tourism revenue, rising youth unemployment and rapid population growth.[3] To date, there are few signs that President Sisi will exercise the political will needed to address these problems.

On the security front, President Sisi's concerted counter-terrorism campaign in the Sinai Peninsula shows few signs of progress in eliminating the very real extremist threat that is sadly on the rise. To the contrary, the military's tactics appear to be further alienating the local population. Increasing the pressure on both the government and its tourism sector, the country's commercial airlines have been struck by two likely terrorist attacks. There have been several assassination attempts on key Egyptian officials, including one that killed state prosecutor Hisham Barakat in 2015[4] and another that narrowly missed then interior minister Mohamed Ibrahim in 2013.[5] It was not so long ago that these types of attacks were unheard of in Egypt. Now there seems to be a steady drumbeat of low level attacks and bombings in major Egyptian cities, including Cairo.

The Egyptian government's response to its security challenges has been heavy handed and clumsy, amounting more to a wholesale crackdown on dissent than an effective effort to root out and interdict extremists. Particularly troubling has been the increase in state-sponsored extrajudicial forced disappearances. In 2015 alone, there were over 1,800 reported cases of

---

[2] http://www.nytimes.com/2016/04/11/world/middleeast/egypt-gives-saudi-arabia-2-islands-in-a-show-of-gratitude.html
[3] http://www.washingtoninstitute.org/policy-analysis/view/will-sisi-squander-his-chance-to-fix-egypts-economy
[4] http://www.aljazeera.com/news/2015/06/egypt-state-prosecutor-motorcade-hit-bomb-attack-cairo-150629083650272.html
[5] http://www.nytimes.com/2013/09/06/world/middleeast/egypts-interior-minister-survives-attack.html

forced disappearances.[6] Mass trials and collective convictions based on vague charges of "harming national interests" have become the norm in Sisi's Egypt, including the recent conviction of 101 people in April who peacefully demonstrated against Egypt giving two Red Sea islands to Saudi Arabia.[7]

Respectfully, this Committee should also be deeply concerned about how Egypt's practice of targeting international organizations attempting to work in Egypt is expanding. Instead of learning a lesson from the international condemnation it received for this practice in 2013, tragically, the Egyptian government appears to be doing precisely the opposite. In 2013, IRI and a select number of other international organizations were the primary focus of the Egyptian security services. The latest Egyptian news reporting suggests that the list of targeted nonprofits and civil society groups has now reached as many as 47 Egyptian and international organizations.[8] A number of international assistance projects have been suspended or cancelled outright. Journalists and academics are routinely being denied entry upon arrival to Egypt.[9] Meanwhile, select Egyptian civil society activists are being arbitrarily denied the freedom to travel outside of Egypt.

Considering the complex challenges the Sisi government faces, it would be tempting to rationalize some of its practices as merely an effort to stabilize the country or "buy time" for later opportunities to take on democratic and civil rights reform. However, the government's actions and rhetoric offer not a single morsel of evidence to support that hopeful notion. Meanwhile, the security situation grows more tenuous and repressive.

RIGHTS AND STABILITY

The tension between rights and stability, an age-old debate this Committee has weighed in many different contexts, should be considered carefully in the case of Egypt. It is my strong belief that counter-terrorism and military operations alone will never be a sufficient or successful response to the genuine extremist threats the country faces. To succeed, Egypt must also enlist the help of its civil society, from the voluntary organizations that address local development issues to the nongovernmental organizations working to promote tolerance, pluralism, women's and minority rights. These groups can help combat the potential appeal of extremist groups and serve as a conduit for citizen input in public policy on issues ranging from health care to economic reform.

---

[6] http://www.independent.co.uk/news/world/africa/egyptian-government-disappears-1840-people-in-just-12-months-ruling-by-fear-a6923671.html
[7] https://www.alaraby.co.uk/english/news/2016/5/14/101-egyptian-demonstrators-given-mass-prison-sentence
[8] http://www.almasryalyoum.com/news/details/913796
[9] http://www.middleeasteye.net/fr/news/egypt-visa-denied-entry-researcher-husband-airport-229892418

Vibrant civil society institutions can turn citizen frustration into citizen hope, and hope is the greatest prevention to the anger and despair that extremists so often exploit.

Unfortunately, instead of perceiving Egypt's once vibrant civil society as an ally, the Sisi government has steadily narrowed the space in which civil groups are permitted to operate. For example, a 2013 anti-protest law significantly curtails citizens' ability to participate in peaceful public meetings and assembly. It requires a permit from the Ministry of Interior for public meetings of more than 10 persons and carries punishments of up to five years in prison and fines for violations deemed to harm Egypt's broadly defined "national security."[10] The 2015 counter-terrorism law provides stiff penalties for journalists who report on terrorist acts in a way that deviates from the official government narrative.[11] An amendment to Egypt's penal code criminalizes organizations that receive foreign funding with a possible life sentence in instances where foreign funding is being used to undermine "unity."[12] Egypt's Parliament is also drafting a draconian new cybercrime law that provides harsh punishments for similarly vague violations of national security.[13]

Egypt's intensifying crackdown on civil society in the name of stability is, in reality, a step in the opposite direction. In the long term, it will likely increase instability and tension, stifle constructive dissent and drive the desperately disaffected into the shadows -- or worse yet, into the audiences for extremist voices. It's not hard to see parallels in today's conditions to the sweeping sense of marginalization and alienation that fueled mass protests in 2011.

President Sisi himself perhaps best characterizes the crackdown on civil society as "fourth-generation" warfare[14], the nonsensical idea that media and civil society organizations maliciously conspire to undermine people's trust in their government leaders. In this way of thinking, opinions deviating from the government narrative constitute warfare against the Egyptian state. An example of this mindset can be seen in recent comments from Egypt's speaker of parliament, Ali Abdel Aal, about "anti-national research centers." He suggested that such centers organize courses to disrupt state institutions as part of a foreign campaign against Egypt's parliament.[15]

---

[10] https://www.hrw.org/news/2013/11/26/egypt-deeply-restrictive-new-assembly-law

[11] https://freedomhouse.org/report/freedom-press/2016/egypt

[12] https://www.theguardian.com/world/2014/sep/24/egypt-human-rights-crackdown-foreign-funding

[13] http://www.al-monitor.com/pulse/originals/2016/06/egypt-enacts-cyber-crime-law-preserve-national-security.html

[14] https://www.washingtonpost.com/opinions/america-gives-egypt-free-armored-vehicles-and-money-egypt-gives-america-a-slap-in-the-face/2016/05/29/b4f5376c-235b-11c6-8690-f14ca9de2972_story.html

[15] http://english.ahram.org.eg/NewsContent/1/64/217861/Egypt/Politics-/Egypt-parliaments-speaker-attacks-research-centres.aspx?utm_content=buffer41ddf&utm_medium=social&utm_source=twitter.com&utm_campaign=buffer

It might be tempting to dismiss this type of rhetoric as harmless political discourse common to Egypt. History tells us, however, that when conspiracy theory becomes official policy, it has concrete consequences for U.S. interests. For example, consider the absurdity of official statements made by government representatives during the "foreign funding trial" (case 173/2011). The court testimony of Faiza Abu Naga, now a national security advisor to President Sisi, was little more than a stream of baseless ramblings that international democracy and human rights programs were designed to improve relations with "Jewish lobbyists" and are "serving Israeli interests."[16] The judge's opinion in the case was hardly better. He contended the organizations were "a new form of dominance and hegemony, because it is a soft form of colonialism less costly as a means of resistance than the military weapons." He also suggested that these activities are "practiced by the donor countries to disrupt the security and stability of the recipient countries for the purpose of weakening and dismantling them." In that case, as you will recall, without any real evidence, guilty verdicts were handed down for 43 staff from IRI, NDI, Freedom House, ICFJ and KAS together with sentences of up to five years imprisonment and hard labor.

The guilty verdicts, no matter how baseless and politically motivated, continue to affect these staff. They are unable to travel to certain countries for fear of detention or extradition. Some Egyptian local staff have been separated from their families in Egypt for more than three years. Those same staff fear their families inside Egypt will be subjected to intimidation by security services. One IRI staff member was arrested while on travel in Europe, while another's asylum application has remained pending in the U.S. asylum process for more than three years.

Instead of working to resolve this blight on the U.S-Egypt bilateral relationship, the Egyptian government is doubling down on its approach. Reports suggest that Egypt is re-opening and widening the "foreign funding trial" (case 173/2011). It is now arbitrarily targeting a growing number of Egyptian nongovernmental organizations. As many as 47 Egyptian organizations may now be under investigation in this case[17] and formal charges have already been brought against prominent personalities like Mohamed Zaree from the Cairo Institute for Human Rights, Gamal Eid from the Arabic Network for Human Rights Information, and Hossam Baghat from the Egyptian Initiative for Personal Rights.[18] Trial delays have effectively left these individuals in a state of legal limbo and their passports have been confiscated.[19] It is obvious these delays and abuses are aimed at intimidating and silencing independent civil society.

---

[16] http://www.nytimes.com/2014/11/06/world/middleeast/egypt-elevates-fayza-abul-naga-an-official-hostile-to-us.html?_r=1
[17] http://www.almasryalyoum.com/news/details/913796
[18] http://af.reuters.com/article/commoditiesNews/idAFL5N18N4P6
[19] http://af.reuters.com/article/commoditiesNews/idAFL5N18N4P6

EGYPTIAN PERSERVERENCE

Despite the bleak situation existing inside Egypt, IRI and other international organizations remain committed to advancing democratic principles in that once-great country. This is true even though the 2013 guilty verdicts have forced us to take training and skills building programs with Egyptians offshore to third country locations.

Despite the obvious difficulties we face, you might be surprised to learn that these programs remain highly desired by Egyptian reformers. IRI continues its activities to empower Egyptian civil society and political party leaders, though training participants have become accustomed to harassment and on occasion have been outright prevented from attending IRI's workshops. Though the project design is different, the focal point of IRI's approach to Egypt remains unchanged: to assist Egyptian civil society and political party democratic reformers to take part in Egypt's democratic processes. We work to teach skills in coalition-building, participating in public policy debates and issue advocacy to relevant decision makers within formalized institutions. Citizen interaction with formalized institutions like parliament and government ministries is paramount if Egypt is to achieve stability and combat the appeal that extremism feeds on when individuals, especially youth, feel alienated.

We are heartened that, despite the challenges facing democratic actors in Egypt, a recent independent evaluation of IRI's program found promising results that provide a strong impetus for continued engagement. Egyptian participants perceive the offshore model as effective, especially in terms of creating a safe and neutral space for interaction and learning, a model that they believe is not presently feasible inside Egypt. Participants view the skills they learn as support for their efforts at incremental democratic reform. The external evaluation also verified that the safe learning environment has engendered collaboration amongst participants, and that participants have shared their experiences and newfound skills with colleagues in Egypt upon their return.

For these reasons, IRI aims to continue its efforts to assist democratic development in Egypt, despite how unlikely a democratic breakthrough may seem in the foreseeable future.

RECOMMENDATIONS

Madam Chairman, I respectfully offer the following recommendations for the Subcommittee to consider as they pertain to Egypt.

First, a significant backlog of U.S. foreign assistance funds tied to Egypt exists, primarily due to Egyptian obstinacy. I have heard from knowledgeable stakeholders that Egypt's refusal to permit U.S. programming in a wide variety of development sectors has caused a backlog of between $500 and $700 million in unspent or unobligated funds. In the current budget environment where resources are constrained, a significant portion of these funds can be better utilized elsewhere. In Tunisia, for example, significant democratic strides are being made and deserve additional support. This is especially true with respect to programs designed to build democratic institutions and deliver good governance.

Second, continued support for democratic development in Egypt is best accomplished through programs that engage democratic actors and build their skills to make notable contributions in a future democratic breakthrough. These efforts should be consistent with U.S. Law as stipulated in the Brownback Amendment and should be undertaken without pre-approval from the Egyptian government. Given the recent history, it is imperative that U.S. democracy assistance is not subject to an Egyptian government veto.

Finally, U.S. Administration officials, Members of Congress and their staff at every level should raise the "foreign funding" case 173/1000 in every engagement they have with Egyptian officials. These U.S. leaders should deliver a consistent message: insist that re-opening the case and expanding it to include other organizations is unconditionally and unreservedly unacceptable and must be stopped; and, insist that the only solution to the 2013 verdict that convicted 43 staff from international organizations is a full pardon by President Sisi. IRI has carefully examined the president's legal authority to grant pardons and has determined under advisement from legal counsel that no constitutional or legal impediment exists to prevent Sisi from issuing full pardons to IRI and the other NGO staff.

CONCLUSION

Chairman Ros-Lehtinen, Members of the Committee, I offer my sincere thanks for the opportunity to testify on this timely and consequential topic before you today. I wish I could offer a more optimistic testimony, but the importance of Egypt in the region, the significance of the U.S.-Egypt relationship, and the depressing state of affairs within Egypt right now demands that I present this sobering picture. A recent *Economist* article suggested that if Egypt does well, it can lift the region, whereas its collapse would represent a threat to the entire Middle East and Europe.[20] I would add the United States to that list, too.

---

[20] http://www.economist.com/news/special-report/21698436-endless-obstacles-political-freedom-remain-what-arabic-democracy

Ms. Ros-Lehtinen. Very good. Thank you, Ambassador Green. Mr. Awad.

STATEMENT OF MR. MOKHTAR AWAD, RESEARCH FELLOW, PROGRAM ON EXTREMISM, CENTER FOR CYBER AND HOME-LAND SECURITY, GEORGE WASHINGTON UNIVERSITY

Mr. Awad. Madam Chairperson, Ranking Member Deutch, members of the subcommittee, thank you for this opportunity to be here to talk about security in Egypt. In fact, I have recently returned from a long research trip to that country where we have met with colleagues, top security officials, and went to areas like the Western Desert and Suez Canal area to see the situation there on the ground for ourselves. I am going to provide a threat assessment of the situation in Egypt with some relevant recommendations.

The most important thing to understand is that Egypt is facing what is the deadliest and most lethal, complex insurgency in its modern history. Since the Muslim Brotherhood was ousted from power in July 2013, at least 900 security service members lost their lives to an array of terrorist groups seeking to topple the government. The threat in Egypt comes from three different geographic theaters and three different types of groups.

First, there is northeastern Sinai where Islamic State-affiliated militants wage insurgency against the Egyptian Government and poses severe threat to Egypt and Israel.

The second is in the Nile Valley, the heart of Egypt, where 97 percent of the population lives. There, also Islamic State-affiliated elements, some al-Qaeda elements, although small in number, and other violent Islamist groups suspected to be affiliated with some members inside the Muslim Brotherhood, also seek to topple the government there.

Finally, the Western Desert with the vast border with Libya, the Islamic State is attempting to build a presence there.

Let me focus a little bit on the situation in Sinai. You will find in my written testimony detailed information on the Nile Valley and the Western Desert. The situation in the Sinai continues to be quite challenging. Since the fall of 2014, the local jihadist group called Ansar Bayt al-Maqdis, or the Champions or Supporters of Jerusalem, saw its capabilities increase significantly as it pledged allegiance to the Islamic State. Since then, they were able to launch large-scale defensives on the ground, culminating in a July 1, 2015, attack that attempted to hold parts of the city called Sheikh Zuweid in North Sinai. Only after a 12-hour-plus battle and the intervention of Egyptian F-16s was the jihadist threat neutralized.

Since then, Egyptians launched a massive counteroffensive that has had some successes. It should be noted that the jihadists in North Sinai do not control any population centers. Also, their areas of operation have largely been contained. Despite these successes, they have shifted their tactics and have used more IEDs and focused on terrorist attacks like the downing of the Russian airliner in October 2015. As a result, the first quarter of 2016 is the deadliest 3 months on record for Egyptian troops in North Sinai. The frequency of attacks has also increased, but again, they have not been back to the same quality of capabilities that they had prior to July.

Quickly, on the Nile Valley and the Western Desert, the most important things to understand there is that the situation is comparatively better compared to the Sinai. With that being said, although the government has had great successes in the Nile Valley, cracking down on some of the violent Islamists connected to the Muslim Brotherhood and al-Qaeda, the Islamic state has recently been attempting to bring armed insurgency closer to Cairo. However, these attempts have been thus far checked.

And finally, of course, in the Western Desert smugglers continue to operate, and as pressure increases against the Islamic State in Libya, they are more likely going to look more into the Western Desert to find ways to entrench themselves there.

Finally, let me offer some recommendations. I think for these reasons a continued security relationship with Egypt is of course important for U.S. strategic interests in the region. However, the relationship should reflect the changing nature of the challenges Egypt faces in confronting asymmetric threats from non-state actors and advance U.S. interests. The Obama administration announced that starting in Fiscal Year 2018 the U.S. will channel FMF funds toward procurement in four categories. Counterterrorism, border, maritime, and Sinai security is a good basis for the future of the FMF program. This pathway for updating U.S.-Egypt cooperation is sound and will require close coordination and support between Congress and the administration in order to implement it effectively.

The U.S.-Egypt relationship requires new anchors that go beyond security but also requires updating the security relationship. It should be built on mutual trust, respect, and frankness. The United States should encourage Cairo to implement a comprehensive counterinsurgency strategy in the Sinai that integrates technologies and training with economic development and tribal outreach in order to effectively defeat terrorist elements, all while minimizing collateral damage. Both governments should ensure that defense officials are able to discuss issues related to counterinsurgency frankly and be granted the access necessary to adequately provide training and assistance.

More cooperation is also needed with Egypt's General Intelligence Directorate and to the Ministry of Interior, specifically the State Security. These institutions are key actors in Egypt's fight against terror and thus warrant this further engagement.

Egypt should implement a comprehensive counterterrorism and countering violent extremism strategy that in part cracks down on human rights abuses and improves conditions in prisons to combat radicalization. All assistant should be on the basis of advancing U.S. interests in providing the necessary weapons and training that can help Egypt address its security challenges in ways that align with U.S. interests and values.

Finally, U. S. security cooperation and assistance with Egypt should be conditioned on Egypt's performance in the security field itself instead of political and economic reforms. I look forward to getting into more details in the Q&A. Thank you.

[The prepared statement of Mr. Awad follows:]

Program on Extremism

THE GEORGE WASHINGTON UNIVERSITY

Egypt: Challenges and Opportunities for U.S. Policy

Written Testimony of:

Mokhtar Awad
Research Fellow, Program on Extremism
Center for Cyber and Homeland Security
George Washington University

**Before the U.S. House of Representatives Foreign Affairs Committee,
Subcommittee on Middle East and North Africa**

June 15, 2016

Program on Extremism   t 202-994-2437

2000 Pennsylvania Avenue, NW   f 202-994-2543

Suite 2210   extremism@gwu.edu

Washington, DC 20052   www.cchs.gwu.edu/program-extremism

Madame Chairperson, Ranking Member Deutch, and members of the subcommittee, thank you for the opportunity to appear before you today to discuss the security situation in Egypt.

Egypt has been one of our long standing partners in the Middle East for more than three decades. Its peace with Israel, which was brokered by the U.S., remains one of America's notable successes in this turbulent region as it closed a chapter on a devastating era of large conventional wars between Israel and its neighboring states. In addition to providing overflight rights to U.S. military aircraft and preferential access to U.S. Navy ships through the Suez Canal, Egypt has maintained its peace with Israel. Unlike some other countries in the region, Egypt has not been a state sponsor of terror. Egypt has also been the recipient of U.S. Foreign Military Financing (FMF) for over 30 years and currently receives $1.3 billion annually, and roughly 50 percent of its arsenal is supplied by the United States.

However, Egypt and the region have undergone fundamental changes that have shifted the underlying strategic rationale for this important relationship. The threat arising from the Arab World is no longer coming from conventional wars, but rather in large part from non-state actors deploying terrorism and asymmetric warfare to destabilize states and hold territory in ungoverned spaces. Egypt is increasingly facing such new threats as the country continues to adjust to a new political reality following five years of political upheaval and overwhelming demographic and economic pressures. As a result, the United States and Egypt have struggled to adjust to new regional realities and craft a new strategic rationale for the relationship that is relevant to meet the challenges and threats of the 21st century.

The United States and Egypt need to build new anchors for the bilateral relationship. These anchors should center on upgrading the security relationship, which remains the top priority, but we also need to work together to find new constructive approaches on economic and governance reforms vital for Egypt's continued stability and in ensuring dignity and economic opportunity for 90 million Egyptians, whose ranks grow roughly by 1 million people every six months.

As I wrote with Brian Katulis in a Center for American Progress report last year, both countries should heavily invest in continuing a serious strategic dialogue on issues of mutual concern, focus on expanding contacts between citizens, and look for ways to expand multilateral support for Egypt by coordinating with partners such as the United Arab Emirates, Saudi Arabia, and Egypt's European friends.[1] The new anchors should focus on ways to update the security relationship, open up a dialogue on the need for pluralism and political reform in Egypt, and finally, organize multilateral reform efforts that can help sustain Egypt's economy.

My testimony today will focus on how to update the security relationship in a way that best meets Egypt's new security challenges and U.S. priorities in the region. I hope that success in this area can help rebuild trust in the relationship and produce positive externalities into other areas in the bilateral relationship. Despite the overwhelming challenges in the relationship, Egypt remains one of the few stable countries in the region that has institutions with which we can engage. This is a radically different reality from failed states like Libya, Syria, and Yemen. More importantly, helping Egypt address its security challenges in ways that align with U.S. interests and values will have a tremendously positive impact on stability in Egypt and the wider region. Congress will play an important role in this process of updating our relationship with Egypt and it should work with all of the key agencies of the U.S. administration involved in this relationship to send a unified message to Egypt.

I have structured my testimony today around two main topics:

1. A threat assessment outlining the security challenges that Egypt faces.
2. A set of recommendations for U.S. policy.

Egypt's Threat Assessment:

It is important to first understand the reality of the terrorist threat that Egypt faces today. Immediately following the ouster of the Muslim Brotherhood from power in July 2013, a diverse array of violent Islamist groups stepped up their activities aimed at destabilizing the new government. Over 900 security servicemen have lost their lives to Islamist violence since then, making it the deadliest Islamist insurgency in the country's modern history.

The threat to Egypt comes from three different geographic theatres – the Sinai, the Nile Valley, and the Western Desert – and three different types of actors – Salafi Jihadists affiliated with the Islamic State, others who are with or lean towards Al Qaeda, and a new category of violent Islamists affiliated with some factions inside the Muslim Brotherhood and allied Islamists.

The Sinai Threat:

First, in the northeastern corner of North Sinai governorate, somewhere between 700 to 1000 Islamic State affiliated fighters wage insurgency against the Egyptian military and launch terrorist attacks, of which some are directed at Israel. The main group, Ansar Bayt al-Maqdis, or Supporters of Jerusalem, launched several attacks against Israel and a pipeline that fed Egyptian gas to Israel in 2011-2012.[2] Following former President Mohamed Morsi's ouster in July 2013, the group escalated its attacks against Egyptian security forces in the Sinai, and used sleeper cells they had developed since 2011 in the Egyptian Nile Valley to launch attacks outside the Sinai. Since the fall of 2014, the group's capabilities and the lethality of its attacks significantly increased as it pledged allegiance to the Islamic State group and changed its name to Wilayat Sinai, or Sinai Province. However, despite what the name may imply, the group does not control any population centers and does not exercise governance over any significant territory as the Islamic State does in Syria, Iraq, and Libya.

The so-called Wilayat Sinai was able to launch several large scale ground offensives against Egyptian security forces in the period from fall 2014 to summer 2015. More advanced anti-tank weapons, such as Russian-made Kornet missiles smuggled from Libya and Sudan, were also increasingly used by the group. These efforts culminated into a massive simultaneous attack on July 1, 2015, that appeared to have a primary goal of holding parts of the North Sinai city of Shiekh Zuwaid. Only after a 12 plus hour battle and the intervention of Egyptian F-16s did the Jihadists retreat. In the following months, Egyptian security forces launched a major campaign that seemed to have immediate results in decreasing the number of attacks and casualties. However, the Jihadists adapted tactics and began to rely more heavily on IEDs, use of sleeper cells in cities like Al Arish, and terrorist attacks like the downing of the Russian airliner in October 2015.

As a result, the first quarter of 2016 has been the deadliest for Egyptian troops in North Sinai since 2014 and the frequency of attacks has increased (see figures A and b). Despite this, the Jihadists do not appear to have regained the same qualitative capabilities that they possessed prior to July 2015 as of yet.

Although the major trouble area has been contained to northeastern Sinai, the Jihadists have demonstrated an ability to plant IEDs in central and western Sinai. They have also copied Islamic State tactics in booby-trapping houses in empty or near empty villages whose residents had fled the fighting, presenting a challenge for advancing Egyptian troops.

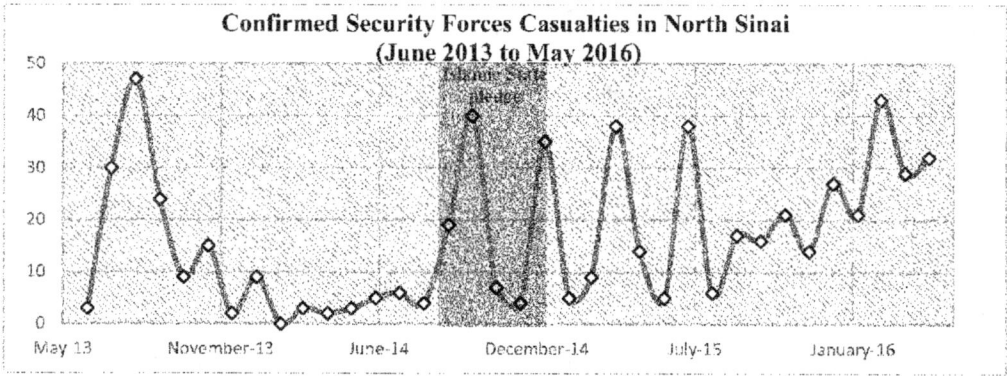

Figure A—Confirmed *Security forces casualties in North Sinai (June 2013 to May 2016). Source: Own database based on official government statements and open source reporting on soldiers' funerals and deaths (approximate).*

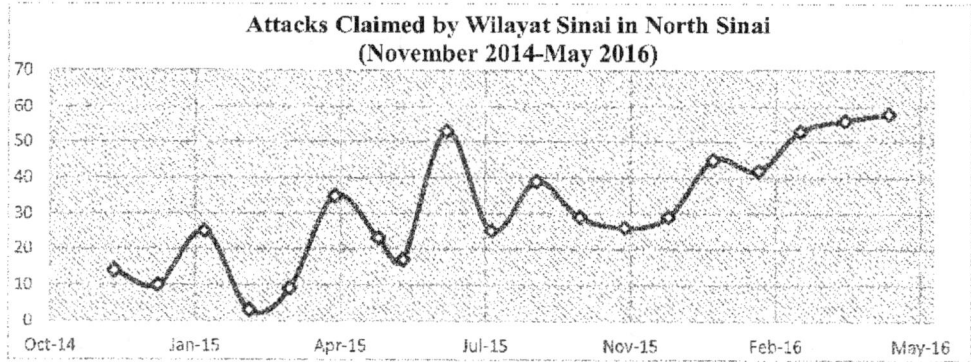

Figure B—*Attacks claimed by Wilayat Sinai in North Sinai. Source: Wilayat Sinai, Islamic State official publications as well as data compiled by analyst Jantzen Garnett. This is not a comprehensive accounting of all attacks and incidents in North Sinai, only those claimed by the group (approximate).*

Although Wilayat Sinai remains relatively contained and isolated geographically, some troubling trends must be monitored closely. The transformation of the group since its pledge of allegiance to the Islamic State in November 2014 makes it one of the most active Islamic State branches. The Islamic State appears to have completely subsumed the local affiliate as its attacks and strategy seem to clearly advance Islamic State core strategic interests.[3] The group's downing of a Russian airliner in October 2015, instantly killing over 200 civilians, is the best demonstration of this as up to that point it had avoided mass civilian casualties. Wilayat Sinai has also been the recipient of material support from the Islamic State core leadership by way of Libya.[4] A network of small fishing boats connects the Northern Sinai coast with Libya's and allows for these transfers. Due to this, the local group may continue to receive material support and other assistance from Islamic State core leadership by way of the sea, even as Egyptian forces may make some gains against it on the ground. The Islamic State looks to this affiliate as both a promising base to attack Egypt and, perhaps more importantly, as a launching pad for attacks against Israel.

The Nile Valley Threat:

Second, there is the Nile Valley, the heart of Egypt where 97 percent of the population lives. Since 2013, some violent Islamist groups believed to be affiliated with certain factions inside the Muslim Brotherhood and other allied Islamists have carried out terrorist attacks against Egyptian security services and acts of sabotage targeting Egypt's infrastructure.[5] Other Salafi Jihadists with Al Qaeda leanings, like the Ajnad Misr group, have also operated there. Finally, the Islamic State has succeeded in infiltrating the Nile Valley by recruiting existing native Salafi Jihadists for its cause and other non-Salafi Jihadists who were engaged with the Muslim Brotherhood affiliated groups.

Despite the great number of threats, the security situation in the Nile Valley is much more stable than North Sinai. This is largely due to work by Egypt's State Security apparatus, which has been able to check violent groups. Egypt's State Security have advantages in the Nile Valley that they lack in other parts of the country, including a deep familiarity of key population centers. An additional reason is that many of the actors they have had to face, especially those affiliated with some inside the Muslim Brotherhood, lack the capacity in terms of strategy and materiel to present a major threat at this time. In the Nile Valley, violence has seen a marked decrease since the summer of 2015 due to security successes and also due to increased fragmentation inside the Muslim Brotherhood.

The Islamic State has demonstrated some signs of trying to make inroads in the Nile Valley and since 2015 has re-activated Salafi Jihadist networks there.[6] They blew up the Italian consulate in Cairo and also attempted to carry out a terror attack at the Karnak Temple in Luxor in the summer of 2015. They have also targeted other government buildings. Most recently, the group has recruited what appears to be Islamist youth in Greater Cairo in an attempt to bring armed insurgency closer to Cairo. These efforts have thus far had limited success due to the strength of Egypt's State Security apparatus and the inexpert nature of the recruits.

The Islamic State appears to be trying to consolidate the fragmented landscape of Nile Valley Islamist militants and simultaneously attempt insurgency in the region while directing terrorist attacks against government, tourist, and other Western interests. The nature of the Nile Valley threat may escalate if the Islamic State—with its expertise, weapons, and financing—succeeds in recruiting more Egyptian Islamists. There are untold thousands of Egyptian Islamist youth who may be susceptible to such recruitment, threatening to turn Egypt into another Tunisia in terms of contributing large numbers of foreign fighters.

Yet at the same time, the ability of the Islamic State to make major gains inside of mainland Egypt in the way that the group has in Syria and Iraq over the past three years is constrained by the simple fact that the sectarianism between Sunni and Shiite groups that drives the conflict in Iraq and Syria is not a factor in Egypt. Furthermore, Egypt lacks easily extractable resources that can finance Islamic State like governance activities. Most importantly, the state is far more cohesive. With that being said, the Islamic State may likely attempt to target Egypt's Christians in an attempt to instigate sectarian strife in areas such as Cairo, Alexandria, and Upper Egypt. Christians are also viewed by Islamists as a legitimate target and Islamic State affiliated elements will view Christians' property and wealth as legitimate financing sources.

Western Desert and Libya Threat:

Finally, there is Egypt's vast Western Desert which shares a more than 1,000 km long border with Libya. Egypt faces threats from weapons smuggled from Libya as well as from the infiltration of Islamic State elements inside its territory. The main threat from the Western Desert was previously criminal networks and smuggling of weapons, but since the rise of Al Qaeda in Eastern Libya and later the Islamic State, Egypt has increasingly focused on terrorist elements spilling over. The government has been able to intercept many weapons shipments, but recognizes that it is not catching all.

Since 2014, Salafi Jihadists have taken an interest in the area and launched some attacks. These groups are primarily interested in securing vital smuggling routes, but also seem to be interested in slowly setting up an infrastructure in the vast desert to be able to launch attacks inside the Nile Valley and more securely link the Libyan and Egyptian theatres. In 2015, the Islamic State officially announced the presence of some of its elements in the Western Desert and decapitated a Bedouin who worked with the government to track smugglers. In the fall of that year Egyptian forces battled Islamic State elements that had infiltrated from Libya and reportedly reached some 30 KM west of Asyut in Upper Egypt.

Egypt also faces an Al Qaeda threat from across the border in the form of Al Murabitun, a terrorist group headed by former Egyptian special forces officer Hisham Ashmawy. Ashmawy used to be a member of Ansar Bayt al Maqdis, but defected due to his refusal to pledge allegiance to the Islamic State. Although his group has not claimed any attacks inside Egypt, it has stated as its objective to topple the government and is attempting to recruit Egyptian Islamists.

Recommendations:

For these reasons, a continued security relationship with Cairo is vital both for U.S. strategic interests and to help ensure the stability of a long time U.S. partner in the region and the Arab World's most populous nation. However, the 20th century strategic rationale for this security relationship is no longer as salient—peace between Egypt and Israel continues not because of U.S. assistance dollars, but because of common interests among actors on the ground. Thus the relationship should reflect the changing nature of the challenges Egypt faces and the wider region in confronting asymmetric threats from non-state actors in the 21st century.

The Obama administration's announcement that starting in Fiscal Year 2018 the U.S. will channel FMF funds towards procurement in four categories—counterterrorism, border security, maritime security, and Sinai security—is a good basis for the future of the FMF program to help advance core U.S. interests in the region and secure Egypt's stability. This pathway for updating U.S.-Egypt cooperation is sound and will require close coordination and support between Congress and the administration in order to implement it effectively.

To help meet these challenges and ensure that the Islamic State does not continue to expand in Egypt, the U.S. and Egypt must both invest in their bilateral relationship. This relationship has witnessed considerable strains and challenges, especially in the past few years, but our significant common interest in fighting terrorism and stabilizing Egypt means that our work together should rest on mutual trust, respect, and frankness. Attempting to leverage the security relationship to force Cairo to implement political and economic reforms will not likely produce the stability and types of economic and political reforms desired and may in fact be counterproductive.

The United States needs to speak frankly with Egypt's leaders about a wide range of concerns including the anti-Americanism prevalent in the Egyptian media and conspiracy theories that the U.S. seeks to destabilize the Egyptian government which Cairo sanctions, serious human rights abuses, and its jailing of non-violent secular activists and artists. Furthermore, the closing down of political space closes off avenues to defeat extremists in the realm of politics and ideas. In fact, some of those who have spoken out against extremists have themselves been jailed, such as anti-Islamist researcher and TV presenter Islam El Beheiry. Unchecked human rights violations and the use of torture in prisons and other detention facilities also contribute to the problem of radicalization. Finally, a free Parliament without the interference of security services is also vital to provide space for open debate on important issues and help build democratic institutions inside Egypt. Failure to address this serious issues ultimately hamper America's ability to develop a new set of anchors to steady its relationship with Egypt, and some of these actions can ultimately undermine stability in Egypt.

But the top priority focus for the United States should be on providing the right set of incentives and disincentives to Egypt so that it can enhance its capacities deal with security threats. U.S. security cooperation and assistance with Egypt should be conditioned on Egypt's performance in that field.

In implementing a more focused security assistance and cooperation program, the United States should encourage Cairo to implement a comprehensive counterinsurgency strategy in the Sinai that integrates technologies and training with economic development and tribal outreach in order to effectively defeat terrorist elements, all while simultaneously minimizing collateral damage. The government in Egypt has taken some steps in this direction, especially in terms of economic development, but it remains to be seen whether these steps are evidence of a coordinated and effective counterinsurgency strategy that aligns with American expectations. Both governments should also ensure that defense officials are able to discuss issues related to counterinsurgency frankly and be granted the access necessary to adequately provide training and assistance.

More cooperation is also needed with Egypt's General Intelligence Directorate and the Ministry of Interior, specifically State Security. These institutions form the backbone of the Egyptian state and most importantly share in devising and implementing Cairo's counterterrorism measures. For these reasons, they warrant greater engagement. Egypt requires a comprehensive counterterrorism strategy and countering violent extremism strategy in its mainland in order to more effectively combat the different strands of Islamist extremists, to make sure Egypt's prisons do not contribute to radicalization, and to prevent Islamist youth from becoming a reservoir of potential Jihadi recruits for either ISIS or Al Qaeda.

Egypt's police, especially those in rural and peripheral areas, requires more training and equipment to be able to ensure basic law and order, and be the first lines of defense against extremists. More intelligence sharing is also needed and frank exchanges of advice and recommendations that help ensure that both countries are more closely aligned in how they combat extremists in the region. High level discussions between Egyptian and American security officials are needed to effectively strategize how both countries can work together and assist one another in combating terrorism.

If indeed Cairo does take concrete steps in aligning its counterinsurgency, counterterrorism, and countering violent extremism strategies with U.S. vision and values, then the FMF program can continue to be of strategic value and benefit for both countries. This will allow for greater exchanges of technologies, training, and provision of weapons that can help Cairo meet these challenges. At the same time, if trust is rebuilt and the security relationship becomes more functional and effective, it could open the pathway to a strategic dialogue on a wider range of issues, including economic and governance reforms.

Sources:

[1] Brian Katulis and Mokhtar Awad, "New Anchors for U.S.-Egypt Relations: Looking to the Future and Learning from the Past 4 Years After Egypt's Revolution," Center for American Progress, January 2015, 9. https://cdn.americanprogress.org/wp-content/uploads/2015/01/EgyptPolicy-report1.pdf

[2] For background see Mokhtar Awad and Samuel Tadros "Bay'a Remorse? Wilayat Sinai and the Nile Valley," CTC Sentinel, August 21, 2015, https://www.ctc.usma.edu/posts/baya-remorse-wilayat-sinai-and-the-nile-valley

[3] For background see Mokhtar Awad, "The Islamic State's foreign policy may be as terrifying as its domestic policy," *Washington Post*, November 13, 2015. https://www.washingtonpost.com/posteverything/wp/2015/11/13/the-islamic-states-foreign-policy-may-be-as-terrifying-as-its-domestic-policy/

[4] See U.S. Treasury Department designation of Libya based Wilayat Sinai member Salmi Salama Salim Sulayman 'Ammar https://www.treasury.gov/press-center/press-releases/Pages/jl0462.aspx

[5] For research documenting the turn to violence by some inside the Muslim Brotherhood, please review: Mokhtar Awad and Mostafa Hashem, *Egypt's Escalating Islamist Insurgency* (Beirut: Carnegie Middle East Center, 2015). http://carnegieendowment.org/files/CMEC_58_Egypt_Awad_Hashem_final.pdf ; Mokhtar Awad, "Egypt's New Radicalism: The Muslim Brotherhood and Jihad," *Foreign Affairs*, February 4, 2016. https://www.foreignaffairs.com/articles/egypt/2016-02-04/egypts-new-radicalism; Mostafa Hashem, "The Great Brotherhood Divide," Sada, March 2, 2016. http://carnegieendowment.org/sada/?fa=62942; Mai Shams El-Din, "Punishing the state: The rise of urban militant cells," Mada Masr, June 10, 2015. http://www.madamasr.com/sections/politics/punishing-state-rise-urban-militant-cells; Mohamed Hamama, "The hidden world of militant 'special committees'," Mada Masr, December 22, 2015. http://www.madamasr.com/sections/politics/hidden-world-militant-special-committees. See also my written testimony to the UK Parliament on the topic http://data.parliament.uk/writtenevidence/committeeevidence.svc/evidencedocument/foreign-affairs-committee/political-islam/written/32560.pdf

[6] Mokhtar Awad, "The Islamic State's Pyramid Scheme: Egyptian Expansion and the Giza Governorate Cell," CTC Sentinel, April 22, 2016, https://www.ctc.usma.edu/posts/the-islamic-states-pyramid-scheme-egyptian-expansion-and-the-giza-governorate-cell

Ms. Ros-Lehtinen. Mr. Awad, thank you so much.
Ms. Hawthorne.

STATEMENT OF MS. AMY HAWTHORNE, DEPUTY DIRECTOR FOR RESEARCH, PROJECT ON MIDDLE EAST DEMOCRACY

Ms. Hawthorne. Good morning. Thank you, Madam Chair, Ranking Member Deutch, distinguished members of the committee. I am honored to be here today to testify alongside my esteemed colleagues.

I would also like to commend the chair and Congressman Connolly for their leadership on a series of crucially important GAO reports that have shed light on U.S. aid to Egypt and for the subcommittee's leadership on holding regular hearings on Egypt over the past few years.

With your permission, I will summarize the key points of my written testimony.

Ms. Ros-Lehtinen. Please do. Thank you so much.

Ms. Hawthorne. Egypt remains important to the United States for all the reasons that have been mentioned this morning, but nearly 3 years after now-President el-Sisi led the military overthrow of Mohamed Morsi's government, Egypt is headed in the wrong direction with regard to political developments, its economy, and its security situation, and in many ways it has become a more difficult partner for the United States. At present, relations with Egypt present more challenges than opportunities for the United States.

With regard to the political situation, as detailed in fact sheets that I attached to my testimony, there is an intense campaign of repression, vast human rights violations and a political crackdown that is far worse than anything that took place under Mubarak or under former President Morsi. I will spare you the details, but suffice it to say that thousands of Egyptians have been locked up, and conditions in detention centers and prisons are thought to involve abuse and torture and the potential radicalization of inmates who are held in these conditions. Civil society and independent human rights groups are under an intense campaign of repression. Blasphemy cases and other prosecution of Egyptians for expressing their opinions and their views, including against Coptic Christians, are at record highs in Sisi's Egypt.

As the leading human rights activist Gamal Eid wrote in a recent article in the New York Times, when independent, political activity and civil society groups are crushed, you run the risk in Egypt of moving toward a situation that was similar to that which existed in Qaddafi's Libya or Saddam Hussein's Iraq in which there are no mediating institutions, no spaces for citizens to gather peacefully and organize and mobilize against their government, and this creates a society that is far more brutal and far less prepared to deal with turbulence and conflict and risks falling into violence.

On the economic front, although President Sisi has a spoken often of improving the economy and the Egyptian Government has taken some important steps, Egypt remains mired in economic problems. By many economic indicators, the economy is getting worse, and most concerning, I don't see a clear sign coming from the Egyptian leadership about a sound economic policy to turn the situation around.

I would also note that one of the key features of Sisi's Egypt, which is an increased role for the military in the civilian economy, is completely antithetical to the development of the competitive, free-market economy that many Egyptians and the U.S. would like to see developed.

With regard to security, my colleague Mokhtar Awad has described the situation far better than I ever could, but I would just like to underscore that there are genuine concerns that Sisi's strategy of combating the real terrorist threat that Egypt faces runs the risk of being so broad and indiscriminate and brutal that it may actually worsen the very problem it is trying to address by expanding the pool of Egyptians aggrieved against their government and susceptible to radicalization.

With regard to U.S. relations, although President Sisi has often said that he seeks a strong relationship and a strategic relationship with the United States, the actions of many in the Egyptian Government suggest otherwise. This is a government that has refused to pardon innocent American citizens who have been wrongly convicted on trumped up charges relating to their work with NGOs; that puts American citizens on trial; that detains American citizens and deports them from the airport with no explanation; that constantly features negative images of and attacks on the United States and its media; and that, as the recent GAO report on security assistance pointed out, refuses to cooperate on many key aspects of U.S. security assistance.

We need to work with Egypt. Although it is not easy, the United States must continue to partner with this government while showing strong signs of concern about the trajectory of the country.

In the question-and-answer, I would be pleased to describe some details about the ways I think we should restructure our ESF and our FMF program in order to develop a course correction with regard to our policies in Egypt. Thank you.

[The prepared statement of Ms. Hawthorne follows:]

www.pomed.org | 1611 Connecticut Ave NW, Suite 300 | Washington, DC, 20009

Prepared Statement
by Amy Hawthorne
Deputy Director of Research, Project on Middle East Democracy

for a hearing before the Subcommittee on the Middle East and North Africa
of the Committee on Foreign Affairs
United States House of Representatives
2nd Session, 114th Congress

"Egypt: Challenges and Opportunities for U.S. Policy"
June 15, 2016

Thank you, Madam Chair, Ranking Member Deutch, distinguished Members of the Subcommittee, for inviting me to testify at this hearing entitled "Egypt: Challenges and Opportunities for U.S. Policy." It is an honor to be here with you to discuss this important topic.

Nearly three years after the Egyptian military's July 2013 ouster of Mohamed Morsi from the presidency, an event that many in Egypt and elsewhere hoped would reset the country's failing democratic transition, Egypt is headed in the wrong direction—politically, economically, and security-wise. Under President Abdel Fattah al-Sisi, Egypt has become an extraordinarily repressive and intolerant security state, one that aims to stifle dissent, diminish civilians' roles in governance and expand the role of security agencies, and turn a diverse citizenry into obedient, uniform subjects. The scale of oppression is worse than under Mubarak's three decades of autocratic rule or Morsi's one year in office. Under Sisi, Egypt is also a more difficult partner for the United States in several key respects. At present, there are far more challenges than opportunities for the United States in Egypt.

To some observers, Egypt under Sisi may appear to have achieved a kind of stability through harsh repression. Evidently Sisi retains the support of significant portions of the Egyptian population, and there is no obvious better alternative to his rule at present. Egypt exists in a dangerous and turbulent neighborhood, with threats right on and inside its borders. But many of its current problems are self-inflicted. Moreover, as we have seen in Egypt in recent years, public opinion can be fickle. The policies of the current regime are generating or worsening the conditions that feed broader discontent, the alienation and radicalization of young Egyptians, and future unrest. It is impossible to predict when and how the next wave of popular unrest could come to Egypt, or whether and when Sisi will consolidate his power over what currently is not a fully cohesive set of state institutions. But authoritarian rule imposed in an attempt to control a youthful, economically-marginalized population with unmet aspirations for greater opportunity simply is not sustainable. The Egyptian government's brutal crackdown since 2013 against dissent, peaceful independent political participation, and free expression, combined with terrorism and other security challenges, corruption, government inefficiency and neglect, and worsening economic problems that hit especially hard the tens of millions of Egyptians who live near or below the poverty line, are a recipe for a social explosion at some point in the future.

U.S. Security and Strategic Interests

To be sure, Egypt remains important to the United States, due primarily to its geostrategic location and its large population, which according to recent reports has reached 91 million people--the largest in the Middle East and North Africa. We have to continue to try to work with Egypt to achieve U.S. security goals, including advancing Arab-Israeli peace, defeating ISIS-affiliated groups and other jihadists in the Sinai Peninsula and elsewhere in Egypt, and maintaining strategic privileges provided by Egypt effectively in return for military aid that help the U.S. military project power in the region, such as expedited approval for U.S. overflights and Suez canal passage for our Navy ships. And an Egyptian government that is aligned with our broader regional objectives, such as those regarding Iran, Iraq, and Libya, remains an enduring U.S. interest. The United States should not and cannot walk away from Egypt. As we pursue near-term security cooperation, we must keep in mind the overarching U.S. interest in an Egypt that can achieve lasting, genuine stability and that is not contributing to the problems of terrorism and radicalization plaguing the Middle East.

But any sound U.S. policy must be based on a clear understanding of the hard realities of Egypt today, as well as on a sober assessment of the limitations of U.S.-Egypt relations. Beneath both countries' familiar rhetoric about a "strategic partnership," bilateral ties are increasingly strained in many areas. It would be unwise for the United States to over-invest hopes and resources in Egypt at present. The United States needs urgently to recalibrate its policy toward Egypt to give more weight and attention to the human rights crisis occurring under Sisi and respond to the lack of cooperation from Egypt in several key areas. We should adjust aspects of our economic and military assistance to demonstrate our concerns about the current course on which Sisi is leading the country and to make sure that we are not contributing inadvertently to the problems that Egypt faces. As we work with the government in Cairo on a range of issues, we must also make clear that we cannot have a robust, or even a business-as-usual, relationship with an Egyptian government that treats so many of its own citizens so poorly and that is not a full partner to the United States. This is not just a question of values. There is a genuine risk that the unaccountable security state in Egypt today is unable to address Egypt's urgent social, economic and political challenges productively and may be expanding the pool of

Egyptians susceptible to radicalization and violence --developments that threaten Egypt's stability as well as U.S. interests.

To be sure, Egypt's future is up to Egyptians, and U.S. influence in Egypt is not abundant. Even during the 30-year rule of Hosni Mubarak, it was a myth that the United States had some vast influence over Egyptian domestic politics. And since Mubarak's ouster and the re-ordering of some parts of the power structure, longstanding strains of nationalism and anti-American attitudes in the body politic have strengthened. Sometimes these nationalist sentiments reflect Egyptians' desire for a more "independent" foreign policy following a popular revolt against an autocratic leader who was closely aligned with the West. But more often in the media and other institutions this nationalism takes ugly, backward, even xenophobic forms. Furthermore, since 2011, the drifting apart of the United States and Egypt that began under Mubarak --what the scholar Steven Cook aptly has termed "the long goodbye"--has accelerated. With the main achievement of the bilateral relationship, Egypt-Israeli peace, long solidified and representing an event far in the past for most Egyptians and Americans, no shared larger goal has emerged to re-energize U.S.-Egypt ties with a new sense of purpose. Egypt and the United States at this point have mainly a transactional relationship, marked by a lack of trust and frustrations on both sides.

Yet it would be incorrect to conclude that U.S. influence in Egypt is absent. The United States is the most powerful country in the world and as such, remains Cairo's most important military and political relationship by far. U.S. engagement, assistance policy, diplomatic pressure and overall posture toward Sisi's government will not change Egypt. But a more consistent approach based on correct priorities and that uses what influence we do have wisely could make a positive difference over time; inaction surely will not. If we really care about Egypt not becoming a source of instability and insecurity, we need to send a strong signal of support for the people of Egypt, especially for those citizens who espouse democratic values. We must send a strong signal to the Egyptian government of our doubts and concerns about the current course Egypt is on, and the urgent need for a course correction. To be sure, this will not be easy, and it will require fortitude, perservance, and a long-term view by the United States, and the willingness to tolerate increased tensions in the bilateral relationship. But it is the only responsible policy for the United States.

Some Difficult Realities of Sisi's Egypt

- **Repression and a Human Rights Crisis Far Worse Than Under Morsi or Mubarak**

As the attached POMED fact-sheet describes in more detail, since then-defense minister Sisi removed Morsi from office, the military-backed government has carried out a vast and relentless campaign of repression against its Muslim Brotherhood and other Islamist opponents, secular and liberal activists, university students, journalists, and ordinary citizens caught up in the dragnet. The scale and severity of this campaign, which is not atypical following a military takeover of the political system, goes far beyond what took place under former presidents Morsi or Mubarak and correctly is described as a crisis. Human rights groups report that some 40,000 Egyptians have been arrested since 2013. Many of these people have been locked up for belonging to the now-illegal Muslim Brotherhood, and still others for violating the 2013 protest law, which effectively makes peaceful demonstrations against the government illegal and subject to harsh prison sentences and fines. Thousands of Egyptians have been put on trial and sentenced to prison--and more than 1,000 defendants have been sentenced to death, often in rushed, mass trials--in what credible observers describe as politically-motivated proceedings lacking minimum due process standards. Conditions in detention centers and prisons are very poor, with rising reported incidents of torture, abuse, denial of medical treatment, and overcrowding, and with thousands of Egyptians trapped in pre-trial detention for extended periods without adequate judicial recourse. In the past year, Egyptian human rights groups have raised alarms about what they describe as the emergence of two new systematic policies employed against hundreds of Egyptians by security agencies that are frighteningly reminiscent of practices employed by Moamar Qaddafi in Libya or Saddam Hussein in Iraq—enforced disappearances of activists and extra-judicial killings of alleged government opponents. In one widely-publicized potential example of unaccountable security agencies run amuck, some informed observers believe that security forces may have been involved in the abduction, torture, and killing of Italian doctoral student Guilio Regeni this winter. Egyptian rights researchers report that many such incidents have occurred against their fellow citizens, though with little international attention.

Some of these human rights abuses are being committed as dangerous excesses in Egypt's counter-terrorism campaign. Egypt faces a genuine terrorism threat. But indiscriminate and violent responses by the state risk making the problem even bigger by generating millions of Egyptians who are deeply aggrieved against the government and highly susceptible to radical, violent narratives and recruitment. This is a particular worry in the north Sinai Peninsula, where the Egyptian military is engaged in a difficult campaign against Egyptian jihadists affiliated with the Islamic State –a campaign that to succeed, must gain the trust and cooperation of local Sinai communities to work against the jihadists. Such trust-building continues to be elusive in the face of far-reaching security measures, including destruction of homes, that often hurt the civilian population and breed resentment, and the ongoing state neglect of persistent local demands for better governance, safety, and economic and social inclusion.

But Sisi's crackdown goes far beyond a campaign against jihadists, other radicals, and even his Muslim Brotherhood opponents. It extends to those who are alleged to have challenged official narratives or somehow offended conservative state sensibilities or "public morals." It includes pro-democracy youth who represent potential organizers of peaceful movements and protests of the kind that led to the ouster of Mubarak. Many in the Egyptian leadership apparently see such youth as a major threat to stability and public order and are determined to block a repeat of the January 25 protests. Under Sisi's leadership, state agencies have locked up leading youth activists for "terrorism" or other security threats. In addition, the state has prosecuted record numbers of Coptic Christians, atheists, writers, and others deemed "outside the mainstream" for blasphemy. Perpetrators of communal attacks on Coptic Christians rarely are brought to justice. Egypt is now second only to China in the number of journalists in prison. Art galleries and cafes have been shut down and a new law to tighten controls over social media, one of the remaining spaces for debate and open expression for young Egyptians, is looming.

Finally, the authorities are pursuing a crackdown on human rights organizations. These groups form the core of Egypt's independent civil society and despite intense pressure against them, continue to monitor and document violations, defend victims of abuse, promote accountability, and raise public awareness of international human rights norms and democratic values. As the attached POMED time-line describes, the state has re-opened a nefarious 2011 case under which U.S. and German democracy groups were prosecuted in a systematic attempt to put numerous local (and possibly foreign) NGOs out of business through investigations into illegally receiving foreign funding and other allegations widely seen as baseless. Prominent human rights workers have been interrogated, subject to travel bans and asset freezes without due process, harassed, vilified by the media, and even arrested, with reports of harsh prison treatment for some. Some activists have been forced to flee Egypt after receiving death threats.

If successful, the attempt to crush the human rights movement, along with related moves to eliminate other legitimate independent institutions and otherwise shrink the civic sphere to sanctioned pro-state voices, would be ominous for Egypt's future. Not only would there be no credible indigenous organizations to document and report, for Egyptians and the international community, on developments inside the country. But as the veteran Egyptian human rights campaigner Gamal Eid wrote in the *New York Times* in April, human rights groups and other citizen-based organizations also can serve as crucial mediators between the government and society, helping to articulate citizens' demands and generating constructive solutions for social problems. When this mediating zone is destroyed, as it was in Assad's Syria or Qaddafi's Libya, societies have a much harder time managing conflict and unrest, and violent confrontations and the breakdown of public order become much more likely. Indeed, stifling independent political activity more broadly under the guise of "restoring order" or "protecting state prestige" dangerously closes off channels for peaceful participation and increases resentment against the government. It is worth asking why, when Egypt faces a genuine terrorist threat, so many state resources are being deployed so assiduously against peaceful activists, journalists, and other such citizens. It is also worth asking whether a state carrying out such vast repression will possess the necessary moral authority and legitimacy before key sectors of its own population to succeed in the urgent campaign against the false narrative of the Islamic State.

- **Deepening Economic Challenges**

With its large, youthful population, enviable geographic location close to Europe, sub-Saharan Africa, and the Middle East, and other resources, Egypt has huge economic potential that sadly has never been tapped fully by any of its leaders. President Sisi correctly made getting Egypt's economy back on track after the turmoil of the post-Mubarak era among his first promises to the Egyptian public, pledging to undertake difficult reforms while protecting the poorest, most vulnerable citizens from more hardship. He urged Egyptians to be patient, noting that there are no quick fixes to the country's deep-seated economic problems, and that it might take a few years for improvements to be felt.

Unfortunately, two years into Sisi's presidency, economic challenges are mounting, not easing. Inflation is rising, hitting the pocketbooks of tens of millions of poor Egyptians already struggling to make ends meet. The persistent unemployment crisis continues, by some reports reaching 40 percent among young Egyptian job-seekers. Attempts to revive the tourism industry have floundered in the face of security concerns. Foreign direct investment has not flocked to Egypt at anywhere close to the levels needed, due to worries over security, an uncertain investment climate, and an often poorly-functioning judicial system. Without boosts in these key sources of hard currency, Egypt has had trouble propping up its own currency, continuing to put pressure on its depleted foreign reserves to do so while delaying what may be an inevitable devaluation of the Egyptian Pound.

The government has continued to finance its growing budget deficit through borrowing, siphoning funds from the local banking sector that could be lent more productively to small and medium businesses, and taking on more international debt. Egypt's perennial problem of growing state expenditures, heavily tilted toward costly subsidies and wages and other patronage to key interest groups, and declining revenue, due to weak economic output and insufficient tax income, continues. Increasingly it appears that Egypt is living on borrowed economic time. Egypt has avoided a fiscal and an energy crisis thanks largely to the huge aid packages from wealthy Gulf allies seeking to bolster the post-Morsi order, but it is not certain that such generosity will continue indefinitely. Egypt's large informal economy has provided another cushion against a full-blown crisis, but it too is a poor long-term answer. The informal sector simple cannot provide the stable, well-paying employment needed to absorb enough job-seekers, boost productivity, and widen the state's tax-base.

To be sure, there is no quick fix for Egypt's economic problems, especially the complex one of unemployment, which requires labor market reforms, major changes to the educational system, and boosting different productive sectors and small and medium businesses. But Sisi's government has hesitated even to launch a serious program to fix these and other problems. Indeed, despite government rhetoric, Sisi's commitment to a reform path is uncertain. Many of the government's economic measures are a confusing array of ostensibly pro-reform moves, followed by statist reversals, paralysis, or ministerial shuffles. Some Gulf officials privately express deep frustration with the situation. The reasons for the lack of adequate progress are too many to list here. But they certainly include Sisi's over-reliance on costly but highly dubious mega-projects such as the planned building of a new capital city, at the expense of more urgent and worthwhile investments in human development and basic infrastructure. And the expanding and privileged economic role of the military is antithetical to the development of a more competitive, fair, market-based economy.

The combination of intensifying repression, growing economic hardship, ongoing labor unrest, unmet Mubarak-era demands for social justice, deteriorating state services, and looming needed but unpopular subsidy and other reforms does not bode well for Egypt's stability.

Improving the economy will be arduous for any leader of Egypt. But without a clear vision, social dialogue and buy-in from key constituencies, and adequate safety-valves for dissent, the task becomes even more daunting, and international aid and other offers of support far less useful.

- **Troubling Egyptian Government Attitudes Toward the United States**

Sisi has spoken often of his wish to maintain a "strategic," strong relationship with the United States. The actions of some parts of his government, however, belie this rhetoric. Under Sisi, American citizens have been arrested, put on trial, and imprisoned on politically-motivated charges. For example, civil society activist Aya Hegazi, an Egyptian-American from Virginia, and her husband are standing trial for what many observers describe as trumped-up charges of child abuse while running an NGO that helps Cairo street children. Other U.S. citizens have been deported from Cairo Airport and deemed security risks. Absurd stories describing nefarious U.S. government plots to weaken Egypt through foreign assistance and other "infiltration" and even depicting the United States as an enemy regularly appear in the media, including in the state-owned press. The Egyptian government has obstructed the implementation of economic aid projects for higher education and civil society development, among others, including by refusing to register NGOs responsible for helping to implement such initiatives to benefit Egyptian citizens. Sisi has so far refused U.S. requests to exonerate the employees of U.S. democracy organizations convicted of criminal charges in 2013 on trumped-up allegations in a flawed trial. And as a recent report by the Government Accountability Office (GAO) described, Egyptian officials routinely decline to cooperate with end-use monitoring and human-rights vetting requirements for U.S. security assistance.

Certainly, there are Egyptian officials who appreciate U.S. economic and military aid and who want to work constructively with the United States. But they may not be the most powerful actors in the system at present. And the troubling incidents described above are frequent enough to suggest that Egypt is playing a double game in which its government seeks to keep U.S. aid and other support flowing, on its terms, while targeting U.S. citizens with impunity, obstructing other cooperation, and demonizing the United States to its public. And it suggests that despite a nearly $80 billion investment of U.S. aid in Egypt since the 1970s, and close security ties, the United States does not share values or a worldview with Egypt's leaders.

Also worth noting is Egypt's weakened role in the Middle East and thus its diminished role as a U.S. partner on regional diplomacy. It is a U.S. truism that Egypt is a leader of the Arab world and a key regional actor, heightening its importance as a US ally. But beginning in the late Mubarak era, Egypt diverged from U.S. regional policy on some important issues and saw its influence outside its borders reduced as a result of the stagnation of decades of autocratic rule. Since the 2011 uprising, and continuing under Sisi's presidency, Egypt has turned inward, pre-occupied by turmoil at home and consumed by economic, security, and political challenges on the domestic front. To be sure, Egypt retains weight in the region, but this is nowadays more due to its size and potential for spreading instability beyond its borders than to its ability to project decisive influence in regional affairs. Today, Egypt is less a leading regional actor, problem-solver or exporter of economic dynamism and other public goods than a country whose stability and security is a source of concern to its neighbor Israel and to the present center of gravity in the Arab world, the Gulf countries. Indeed, Egypt currently is a nation that depends on aid from its Gulf allies and others simply to keep its economy afloat.

Recommendations for U.S. Policy

What can and should the United States do to address some of the core challenges of Sisi's Egypt: intense repression and a crackdown on peaceful activism; terrorism involving different radical groups in the Sinai and the Nile Valley; the struggling economy; Egyptian actions against Americans and lack of cooperation on assistance? There is no quick fix that the United States (or any other country) can pursue in Egypt and as described above, U.S. influence is not vast. But a course correction is needed. With a recalibration of U.S. policy to include carefully-targeted, consistently-pursued measures, we stand a better change of exerting a positive influence over time, and at least not inadvertently making these problems worse or even being complicit in the repression. U.S. policy toward Egypt must balance the need for short-term security cooperation with the Egyptian government with attention to the medium-term risks for Egypt's stability if the current intense repression continues and a long-term concern for the welfare of the Egyptian people. Below, I offer a few suggestions for steps that the United States should take in its relations with Egypt to make a course correction, to better balance a range of U.S. interests, and to signal to Sisi that a business-as-usual relationship with Washington is not possible until Egypt moves onto a more constructive path.

- **Human Rights Diplomacy and Supporting Democratic Values**

The United States must make human rights a much higher priority in Egypt. Significant democratic progress is unlikely in the foreseeable future, but it is possible to envision an easing of the human rights crackdown that would relieve pressures in Egyptian society and expand the space for peaceful expression. Our goal should be supporting Egyptians who want a more tolerant, democratic country remain alive and buy time, to help keep open even a small political space for peaceful participation and peaceful change.

U.S. officials across the interagency must speak out in public, not just in private, about the human rights crisis, emphasizing the potential for violent repression to widen the pool of disaffected, aggrieved Egyptian youth and to hinder Egypt's efforts to achieve genuine stability. To be sure, Egypt often lashes out harshly in response to U.S. (and other international) criticism and pressing these issues can add tension to the bilateral relationship. But the United States is always stronger and more respected when we consistently uphold our democratic values and support those Egyptians who share them, and when we take a long view that Egypt's future can be better and that its people deserve far better, even as it is on a worrying path now. While Sisi's government may bitterly complain when the United States raises human rights, even sensitive issues, it is unlikely that Egypt will cease cooperation on core areas of security partnership in response—especially in areas that are fully in Egypt's own interests such as combating the Islamic State. And U.S. human rights concerns are not a "Western imposition" or holding Egypt to unfair Western standards, as Sisi has asserted. Egypt has many human rights provisions enshrined in its 2014 constitution, and is a signatory to key international human rights instruments. Furthermore, Egyptian human rights organizations and the quasi-official National Council for Human Rights monitor and speak out about a range of human rights abuses, and the United States typically is echoing these indigenous concerns. Finally, the argument that Egypt will be more responsive to private diplomacy rather than public criticism is not supported by experience, and can become an excuse for inaction. Egypt remains sensitive to its international image and seeks U.S. and other international endorsement of its political trajectory. There are examples in recent years where the United States has been able to achieve small, yet meaningful, progress on human-rights related issues in Egypt due to a combination of public statements, private pressure, and sustained efforts in coordination with our democratic allies.

The United States should prioritize the following issues in its diplomacy with Egypt:

- Insist that Egypt pardon or otherwise exonerate the 43 employees, including American citizens, of U.S. and German democracy organizations wrongly convicted in 2013 on spurious charges. The United States must make clear that failure to resolve this deeply negative episode in the bilateral relationship will remain an obstacle to stronger relations with Sisi.
- Urge Egypt to drop Case 173 against human rights NGOs and other civil society groups and end harassment of human rights workers and other peaceful activists and allow these organizations to operate and receive foreign funding under internationally-accepted standards of freedom of association and assembly.
- Work with our democratic allies in Europe and elsewhere to raise Egypt's human rights crisis at the session of the UN Human Rights Council (HRC) in Geneva that is now underway, building on important U.S. efforts at the March 2014 session. The HRC represents an important opportunity for the United States to show leadership on this issue and to work with our allies in a multilateral manner on Egypt—which only strengthens our influence. Failure to lead on or join a statement in Geneva would be an important missed opportunity for this administration.
- Press Egypt to improve conditions for detainees and prisons, including by allowing international and local organizations to monitor such conditions, and to improve its policies on pre-trial detention, which has become a means to keep thousands of Egyptians locked up for long periods without due process. Stress to our Egyptian counterparts that torture and other abuse of detainees is very likely to contribute to widespread grievances by citizens against the state and make radicals' recruitment of young Egyptians easier.
- Call for accountability for alleged cases of brutality by security forces and an end to practices of extra-judicial killings and enforced disappearances.
- Urge Sisi to call for a halt to anti-Americanism in the Egyptian media and the unfair deportation, arrest, and trial of U.S. citizens, and make clear that failure to do so will harm the bilateral relationship in material ways.

- **Restructuring Economic Assistance**

It is long past time for an honest rethink of our bilateral economic assistance program. More than $30 billion in economic aid to Egypt since the 1970s has helped Egypt achieved important things, but one need only look at our aid program has fallen far short of the kind of transformative development results that one might have hoped for with such a massive investment over so many years. And, while many Egyptians have benefited from U.S. economic aid programs and appreciate American support, we must be honest that our aid program has not built a wide constituency for the United States in Egypt or been a driver for strong relations with the Egyptian government or citizens across a range of areas. As a recent GAO report noted, there is a large backlog of hundreds of millions of dollars of unspent Economic Support Funds. There are many reasons for this backlog, including bureaucracy in Egypt and sometimes in the United States; a development environment in Egypt that can slow or halt the implementation of projects; an overreliance on the Egyptian government as the overseer or counterpart on many aid projects, as opposed to more robust partnerships with NGOs and the private sector; mismatches in U.S. and Egyptian priorities; turmoil and frequent cabinet and ministerial changes in Egypt since 2011; and last but not least, Egyptian government obstructionism on certain assistance programs through its refusal to register U.S. implementing organizations or other forms of non-cooperation. The assistance relationship is too often dominated by tensions and disagreements rather than cooperation and partnership. Overall, a central problem—not unusual in countries where aid is provided primarily for strategic reasons as opposed to shared values or development opportunities—is that the United States simply does not have a willing development partner in Egypt to the degree desired for greater success. Our goals and priorities are not fully aligned and sometimes it seems that the United States wants certain changes in Egypt more than Egypt does.

We should seek to maintain an economic aid program in Egypt: the solution to these challenges is not to close down the bilateral assistance program, as frustrating as it has become. Egypt still has many development needs, there are still positive contributions that the United States can make to these needs, and it would be shortsighted and possibly dangerous for U.S. interests to provide a massive security aid program to a repressive government in Egypt and nothing for the Egyptian people.

But the United States does need to pursue a significant restructuring of the ESF program, including through the following steps:

- When possible, reprogramming funds in the pipeline for a consolidated set of targeted new projects that directly support the Egyptian people, as opposed to their government, such as through merit-based scholarships and immunization programs and other initiatives to combat public health challenges. Avoid investing more resources in technical assistance programs with the Egyptian government unless commitment and political will are evident. In some cases, it may be necessary or most beneficial to re-allocate funds appropriated for Egypt ESF to other countries, such as Tunisia, that offer much better official cooperation on assistance, are more receptive to U.S. aid, and can make better use of the resources.

- If such reprogramming and reallocation does take place, explain to the Egyptian public why. Not speaking publicly about some of the challenges in the assistance relationship will only leave the door open to those in Egypt who want to disparage the United States and advance a negative, inaccurate narrative.
- Reprogramming obligated funds in the pipeline may be administratively complicated, time-consuming, and disruptive, so focus mainly on targeting current and future year ESF on the areas described above that provide direct, tangible benefits for the Egyptian people.
- Avoid future projects (and consider winding down current projects) that partner with Egyptian government institutions for "democracy" initiatives. Such projects are not only unlikely to achieve any results in the current repressive environment, they are a farce.
- Provide support for human rights groups through multilateral mechanisms such as various United Nations funds.

- **Foreign Military Financing and Military Cooperation**

Key goals of our military aid and security relationship with Egypt must be to help the Egyptian military combat internal terrorist threats from the Islamic State through effective counter-terrorism strategies, not approaches that make these problems worse, and to use U.S.-supplied weapons and other assistance responsibly and in line with human rights guidelines. To this end, the United States should:

- Continue to pursue the restructuring of FMF to focus on four categories related to counter-terrorism and border security and the phasing out of some legacy weapons programs and the cash-flow financing privilege for Egypt by Fiscal Year 2018.
- Implement the recommendations in the recent GAO report concerning the implementation of much stronger safeguards to make sure that US-supplied weapons are not being used in mass human rights violations by Egyptian forces, especially as US shifts its FMF more toward "counterterrorism" and away from legacy programs.
- Press the Egyptian government for the ability to monitor the use of U.S. supplied weapons in the Sinai Peninsula to ensure gross violations of human rights are not occurring.
- As allowed by the Fiscal Year (FY) 2016 appropriations law, withhold 15 percent of FY 2016 FMF due to human rights violations and designate these funds for emergency support for Egyptian human rights defenders under attack by the government, such as through the Lifeline Fund, and for scholarships for Egyptian students.
- Withhold special perks like Excess Defense Articles until improvements occur in Egyptian cooperation on end-use and human-rights monitoring.

Conclusion

The United States cannot make Egypt change course, and we must continue to work with the Egyptian government on a range of security priorities. But U.S. policy must include attention to a range of interests, including human rights, and not become dominated by counter-terrorism cooperation. Egypt is far too large, complex, and important, still, for such an approach, and backing the status quo without question is certain not to lead to positive results for the United States, or Egypt.

www.pomed.org | 1611 Connecticut Ave NW, Suite 300 | Washington DC

Timeline of Egypt Crackdown on NGOs since July 2014

July 18, 2014: The Egyptian government issues a public ultimatum for all NGOs to register under the repressive Mubarak-era Law 84/2002, and threatens criminal prosecution for organizations that fail to register. A strong international response against this move is critical in preventing the immediate implementation of the threat.

Late 2014: An investigative judge appoints a technical committee from the Ministry of Social Solidarity to investigate whether some NGOs are operating without being registered under Law 84/2002, and to examine documents related to foreign funding.

December 5, 2014: Chairman of the Egyptian Democratic Academy Hossam al-Din Ali and his deputy, Ahmed Ghoneim, learn that they are banned from foreign travel (implying they are under criminal investigation). The travel bans are reportedly related to ongoing investigations into foreign funding of NGOs.

March 2015: Investigators summon Egyptian Democratic Academy staff members for interrogation.

May 21, 2015: Prominent human rights lawyer Negad el-Borai, Director of the United Group law firm, is summoned and interrogated by a judge for involvement in drafting a proposed law to counter abuse and torture in prisons, detention centers, and police stations. El-Borai is summoned again five days later.

June 2015: An investigative judge interrogates el-Borai for a third time for his work on a draft anti-torture law.

June-July 2015: Leading independent civil society groups, the Cairo Institute for Human Rights Studies and the Hisham Mubarak Law Center, are informed by the judiciary that they are under investigation; judicial officials refuse to provide any legal justification for the inquiry.

November 8, 2015: Hossam Bahgat, founder of the prominent NGO the Egyptian Initiative for Personal Rights, is detained for two days on charges of "publishing false news aimed at harming national security."

February 17, 2016: Ministry of Health officials issue an order to close the Nadeem Center for the Rehabilitation of Victims of Violence and Torture on the grounds that it is performing unlicensed work. The Nadeem Center refuses this order; it remains nominally open but unable to carry out its usual work.

February 23, 2016: Bahgat and Gamal Eid, founder of the Arabic Network for Human Rights Information, another well-established independent human rights group, are banned from traveling outside of Egypt by an order from Egypt's Prosecutor General.

March 2016: The Egyptian government formally reopens Case 173 to examine the legal status and foreign funding sources of NGOs. The case was initiated in 2011 and led to the 2011 and 2012 investigations, interrogations, and raids of five American and German pro-democracy NGOs in Egypt. Forty-three staff members from these organizations faced criminal trial and were later convicted in 2013.

March 3, 2016: Rights lawyer Negad el-Borai interrogated again over charges of managing an "illegal organization, [and] disturbing public order."

March 13-15, 2016: Three employees of the civil society organization Nazra for Feminist Studies, two employees of the Cairo Institute for Human Rights Studies (CIHRS), and one employee of the United Group are summoned to appear before the investigating judges for interrogation in Case 173.

March 17, 2016: The Egyptian government seeks to freeze all personal assets of Hossam Bahgat and Gamal Eid, along with the assets of Eid's wife and daughter, who is a minor. The defendants were not formally notified of the asset-freeze effort, only learning of their court hearing through media reports.

March 19, 2016: The Cairo Criminal Court postpones its decision on freezing the assets of Bahgat and Eid.

March 20, 2016: Nazra for Feminist Studies staff are summoned for further interrogation.

March 21, 2016: Judge Hesham Abdel Meguid issues a gag order on media coverage of Case 173.

March 24, 2016: A ruling on the freezing of assets of Bahgat and Eid is postponed.

April 5, 2016: Egypt's Ministry of Health attempts to close down the Nadeem Center for the Rehabilitation of Victims of Violence, but is thwarted when the center's staff refuses to leave.

April 20, 2016: The Cairo Criminal Court postpones its ruling on Bahgat and Eid's cases until May 23. Additional defendants are added to the asset-freeze case, including Moustafa Hassan, director of the Hisham Mubarak Law Center; Abdel Hafiz Tayel, Executive Director of the Egyptian Center for the Right to Education; and CIHRS Co-founder Bahey eldin Hassan, his wife and three of his children, and two additional CIHRS staff members.

May 6, 2016: Malek Adly, Legal Director for the Egyptian Center for Economic and Social Rights, is arrested on charges of incitement to overthrow the government after filing a lawsuit to protest the transfer of two Egyptian islands to Saudi Arabia.

April 25, 2016: Ahmed Abdallah, Board Director for the Egyptian Commission for Rights and Freedoms, is arrested at his home, detained, and charged with incitement and terrorism.

May 17, 2016: Negad el-Borai is summoned for interrogation for the fifth time.

May 19, 2016: Mina Thabet, Director of Marginalized Group Programs at the Egyptian Commission for Rights and Freedoms, is arrested at his home, detained, and charged with incitement and terrorism.

May 23, 2016: For the fourth time, the Cairo Criminal Court postpones ruling on the case to freeze the assets of Bahgat, Eid, and the other defendants until July 17.

May 24, 2016: Radwa Ahmed, a lawyer with the Arabic Network for Human Rights Information, is summoned to court by the judge presiding over Case 173.

May 26, 2016: Cairo Airport authorities inform CIHRS Director Mohamed Zaree that he is under investigation and banned from foreign travel.

www.pomed.org | 1611 Connecticut Ave NW, Suite 300 | Washington DC

Egypt Under President Sisi: Worse than Under Mubarak or Morsi

Prison Conditions: **Egypt has arrested more than 40,000 political detainees since mid-2013.** Former Egyptian-American political prisoner Mohamed Soltan has described prisons as "fertile ground for radicalization."

Torture: The El Nadeem Center for the Rehabilitation of Victims of Violence reported 137 deaths **due to torture while in detention** in 2015. Other local organizations have documented hundreds of additional torture cases.

Extrajudicial Killings: Egyptian rights groups documented 754 extrajudicial killings by security forces in 2016.

Forced Disappearances: According to credible local sources, Egypt's state intelligence and security agencies abducted and disappeared **204 people** between December 2015 and March 2016.

Military Courts: In April 2016, Human Rights Watch reported that **military courts have** tried at least **7,420 Egyptian civilians since October 2014** under the courts' expanded authority granted by President Sisi.

Death Sentences: **An estimated 1,700 people have been** sentenced to death since 2014 in what many governments and rights organizations describe as unfair and politically motivated trials lacking due process.

Terrorism Law: The **2015 anti-terrorism law** grants the president, prosecutors, and security agencies broad powers to "ensure public order and security" equivalent to those granted by a state of emergency.

Organized Violent Attacks: **Violent attacks by militant groups have** intensified under Sisi, with attacks occurring in 2015 at a rate more than three times greater than in 2014, and more than 50 times greater than in 2010-2012.

Freedom of Association: Case 173 targeting American and Egyptian staff of IRI, NDI, Freedom House, and two other US and German NGOs, re-opened in 2016, with **dozens of civil society organizations now facing** closure and staff members facing criminal detention, prosecution, travel bans, and asset freezes. Prominent local groups now under investigation include the Egyptian Institute for Personal Rights (EIPR), the Cairo Institute for Human Rights Studies (CIHRS), and the Arab Network for Human Rights Information (ANHRI).

Freedom of Press: Egypt is now **second only to China in the number of journalists in prison**. The Committee to Protect Journalists reported in December 2015 that at least 23 journalists are jailed under the "pretext of national security" on a variety of charges, including spreading false news, illegally protesting, and joining terror groups.

Freedom of Speech: **Blasphemy cases** continue to be prosecuted, targeting authors, poets, and even Coptic Christian teenagers mocking the Islamic State.

Freedom of Assembly: Protests remain illegal under the 2013 demonstrations law, and **hundreds have been** given **lengthy jail terms on protest-related charges,** including prominent activists Ahmed Maher and Alaa Abdelfattah.

Economy: Egypt's **foreign reserves are now** less than half **its 2010 levels.** Youth unemployment stands at 42 percent, with 850,000 new workers entering the job market annually.

Corruption: Egypt's former chief corruption auditor publicly estimated that approximately **$76 billion was siphoned from Egypt's public sector through pervasive corruption** from 2012-2015. He was placed under house arrest in March 2016 and is now being tried on charges of spreading false news and disturbing the peace.

Ms. ROS-LEHTINEN. Thank you so much. Excellent testimony from all three. I will start the question-and-answer period.

Ambassador Green, I completely agree that if the Egyptian Government keeps stifling dissent and does not allow for more citizen participation, it will likely end up destabilizing the country even further.

You mentioned that your legal team had looked into the Egyptian government's authority to issue pardons to the 43 NGO staff, and that you had concluded that it is completely within its power to do so. And when I have raised this issue with Egyptian officials, I have been told that the biggest obstacle is the judiciary's ongoing review and then reform of the penal code, which would then need to be passed by the Parliament. What is your understanding of the judiciary's role in this process, and how can we help Egypt to move these pardons forward and to start seeing civil society as an ally in its development and not as a problem?

Ambassador GREEN. Thank you, Madam Chair, for that question. First off, as you alluded to, our best legal information is that they can move immediately to issue pardons. I would note, as some of you have pointed out, they do not seem to have a barrier in reopening the case in adding defendants. It is only pardoning the convicted that they seem to hesitate over. And again, we simply don't see legal barriers to it. There are more political obstacles that they keep raising.

Madam Chair, I think the best answer to the question that you posed about how to move this forward is really, quite frankly, to continue doing what you have been doing and others on the committee have been doing and that is raise this every single time. Egypt is an important ally, and as an important ally, we need to speak frankly and make it very clear to them at every single possible opportunity that this matters to us. Their treatment of American citizens, as well as citizens of their own country, but particularly American citizens is something that matters to us and we will not let stand, so I think making that case over and over again.

And then finally just on the logical point, as some of you have said, they are making it hard for us to help them. We wish to see, all of us, Egypt succeed. We need Egypt to succeed, and the lessons of our experience as a nation, as well as organizations like NDI and IRI, is that for security to be sustainable, it must involve citizens and civil society.

Ms. ROS-LEHTINEN. Thank you very much, sir.

Mr. Awad, you testified that, relative to the Sinai, the Egyptian security forces have so far been able to frustrate ISIS and other violent groups in the Nile Valley. What elements does Egypt need to include in its counterinsurgency strategy if it is to stop ISIS from expanding further? And what do you see as ISIS' strategy in Egypt as it attempts to link its operations with those in Libya?

Mr. AWAD. So let me discuss the situation in the Sinai. Counterinsurgency really relates to the Sinai. The issue is that the Egyptian Government and the military has articulated different parts of the strategy: Economic development, tribal outreach in an informal way, and beginning to update some of the doctrine and integrating intelligence surveillance and reconnaissance methods and how they are fighting the terrorists.

The problem is, thus far, we don't necessarily see a unified central command that is implementing a counterinsurgency strategy. Different parts, again, are articulated. There is supposed to be a command that is for countering terrorism and economic development of the Sinai. However, it remains to be seen if in fact we will see the Egyptian Government saying that it is going to do counterinsurgency. The problem is some officials don't even like the term insurgency, but that is a whole other set of issues.

When it comes to the Islamic State, as I have written in the West Point Sentinel in multiple articles, the Islamic State looks at Egypt as, most importantly, a base of operations that can be used to launch attacks against Israel. This is the case of the Sinai. Also, it can link the Sinai in the Libyan theater, so being able to have assets in the Western Desert that can secure the smuggling routes. Being able to have access to the Nile Valley that can continue that route from the Western Desert to Sinai is key and vital. Egypt also has a lot of Western interests, tourist targets, so Islamic State looks at it as a place where it can do external operations against Western targets.

Finally, Egypt is an untapped reservoir, from their perspective, of recruits. We look at tiny Tunisia and the thousands of people it exported to that group, whereas in Egypt only a fraction of that number. So the Islamic State is looking to try and recruit as much as possible inside Egypt to feed its different branches but also to increase its operations in Egypt proper.

Ms. ROS-LEHTINEN. Thank you very much. Thank you.

Mr. Deutch is recognized.

Mr. DEUTCH. Thank you, Madam Chairman.

We have had a lot of discussion about the security issue and the human rights issue and how to bridge them, and I wanted to come at this a different way. President Sisi has taken a leading role in countering violent Islamic extremism, and his has been a needed and welcomed voice in the region. The question, though, is not about how we perceive it. The question is how do the Egyptian people perceive it, number one. And given the crackdown on Islamists, is President Sisi able to be a voice of influence in the broader region? Ms. Hawthorne?

Ms. HAWTHORNE. Thank you. That is a crucial question. I believe that many Egyptians do support President Sisi's approach, and he does continue to enjoy support from large parts of the Egyptian population. But first of all, that support has notably declined in the past year as problems in Egypt have mounted.

And secondly, I believe there are many Egyptians who are very worried and fearful of President Sisi's counterterrorism approach. In fact, many of these Egyptians are the very ones who the government and state institutions need to be able to reach to convince them not to turn to violence, not to turn to radicalization. And it is this constituency of Egyptian citizens who themselves or their friends or their families have been arrested, detained, tortured, subject to other kinds of mistreatment, convicted in trials that lack any semblance of due process. I think for those Egyptians they are looking for Egyptian leadership that has the moral authority to talk about values of tolerance and acceptance and human rights that are at the core of countering any message from ISIS. And they have, I think, a very serious concern.

President Sisi speaks out against Islamic radicalism, which is crucial, but the other half of the equation, which is all of the other things that are needed to diminish the appeal of these groups, is really missing at this time.

Mr. DEUTCH. Thank you. Mr. Awad, can you just follow up? I understand—and we have spoken about the concerns that so many of us share on the human rights front and on civil society, and clearly for those segments of Egyptian society who are trying to express themselves, we understand those problems. But more broadly throughout the region is the position that President Sisi has taken, speaking out against these radical Islamist views, how is that being received, again, throughout the broader region, understanding that there are human rights issues, there are civil society issues throughout the broader region as well, which we have to talk about. But just specifically on his willingness to speak out like this, Mr. Awad, what impact is that having?

Mr. AWAD. Well, we can't say that there is much impact. However, I can say that definitely people across the region appreciated the rhetoric coming from the President of a major country in the Arab world to speak in such frank terms against Islamic extremism and against many of these extremists.

However, for Egypt to have impact, it will have to lead by example. This is not necessarily something that we have seen. Again, we have seen parts of a strategy articulated when it comes to countering violent extremism or CVE, but the government hasn't completely established a unified strategy that can set an example for less stable countries to follow or aspire to.

Mr. DEUTCH. Ambassador Green, again, getting back to human rights and civil society, the frustration that we have expressed—and again, it is an issue I think Mr. Connolly talked about, the expectations that we have. But again, instead of just viewing this as what we expect and how Egypt receives the message that we are sending to them, how do we speak to Egyptian leaders about human rights in a way that resonates with them and that aligns with their interests? Is there a way to do that?

Ambassador GREEN. I think the way that we do that is that we suggest to them over and over again—and we have plenty of lessons to point to—that in the long run, for security to be sustainable, it must have citizen buy-in, particularly from the next generation. Young people have to have a stake in a vibrant Egyptian culture and government, and that means that there has to be a space for citizens to engage and have a voice in their government. That, I think, is what we talk about over and over again.

And if I might, just to add on to what we have just heard from your previous question, Egypt is clearly important to America's interests and to the interests of many in the region. However, I think everyone recognizes that Egypt's economy, as bad as it is, would be even more horrendous if it were not for it being buffeted and held up by outside assistance. And the same thing is true with the military.

So while there is stability in one sense, I think many recognize that in so many ways it is hollow, that unless they make these investments in some kind of citizen engagement, they can never truly and sustainably be secure and have that bright future that everyone of us wants to see.

Mr. DEUTCH. Thank you. Thank you, Madam Chairman.

Ms. ROS-LEHTINEN. Thank you, Mr. Deutch.

Mr. Wilson of South Carolina.

Mr. WILSON OF SOUTH CAROLINA. Thank you, Madam Chairwoman.

Ambassador Green, thank you very much for your service, and I am really so pleased about your presidency of IRI, the International Republican Institute. I wish more American people knew about IRI, also the National Democratic Institute. It is a great example of working together, both parties, promoting democracy around the world.

And I had the opportunity 26 years ago—it was life-changing to me—to be an election observer as a State Senator in Bulgaria June 10, 1990. I will never forget it. It was extraordinary to see the country come to life after fascism, Nazism, communism. And then it gave me the opportunity to invite—and I had a Member of Parliament Stefan Stoyonov and Ambassador Elena Poptodorova come and observe our election. So it was eye-opening.

And then I had the opportunity, due to IRI, to visit in Bratislava, Slovakia; to Novosibirsk, Siberia. What a difference you make. And I had the great opportunity to have Ambassador Peter Burian as an election observer from Slovakia in South Carolina of all things where he unjustly accused me of arranging for half of the voters to have Slovak heritage. It was just a coincidence as we were at the polling locations. But what a difference IRI makes. So thank you.

In your written testimony, you stated that President Sisi's concerted counterterrorism campaign in the Sinai shows few signs of progress in eliminating the very real extremist threat that is sadly on the rise. Based on this observation, could you explain the impact of the really bizarre reports that the U.S. may be withdrawing from the Sinai, and what would that do to the prospect of destroying ISIL/Daesh on the Sinai Peninsula?

Ambassador GREEN. Thank you, Congressman. Thank you for the kind words. And as you know, IRI and NDI are joined at the hip. We are sister organizations working closely together.

I am not sure I am qualified to give you a thorough assessment on the security front, but I would say that we do believe the U.S. must stay engaged with Egypt. It is a crucial partner of ours in the region, so I would certainly not suggest withdrawal in any way, shape, or form.

Mr. WILSON OF SOUTH CAROLINA. Well, to me it is very clear. We either stop ISIL/Daesh overseas or we will see them again here, as Congressman Rohrabacher has so eloquently pointed out.

Mr. Awad, how would you characterize the impact of U.S. military assistance to Egypt? Has it been used effectively?

Mr. AWAD. If I may just to comment on the issue of the MFO in North Sinai——

Mr. WILSON OF SOUTH CAROLINA. Yes, please.

Mr. AWAD [continuing]. Our troops are not there to fight ISIS, so the issue of removal is not taking them out of Egypt necessarily but a more secure location in the South Sinai so it won't have necessarily a negative impact on the fight against ISIS. The troops are there to observe the peace treaty between Egypt and Israel, and that is no longer as acute of a problem as it used to be. So it is for our troops' protection. We are not removing our people from Egypt or we are not limiting the pressure that is applied against the Islamic State there.

For the most part I think there is room for improvement when it comes to how our military assistance is lining up with Egyptian priorities and how that is advancing our point of view toward counterinsurgency in a place like Sinai. When it comes to the use of Apaches, F-16s, they have been effective, as I have noted, as the situation escalated in the Sinai. It is not so much an issue of the major weapons systems that we provide them but how best to provide them ISR-related technologies, drones, and things along those lines, but at the same time ensuring that they will be used in an effective strategy.

So we have made some gains. It is doing some work, but there is a lot that can be done with the type of weapons that we give them. But at the end of the day there needs to be an effective counterinsurgency strategy, an articulated strategy that we can actually latch onto and provide the necessary equipment for.

Mr. WILSON OF SOUTH CAROLINA. Thank you very much. And, Ambassador Green, how could you explain, sadly, the relatively low voter turnout in Egypt selections? What can the United States do to encourage greater participation in the political process?

Ambassador GREEN. Well, obviously, the most important things that can be done are by the Egyptian Government itself. It is creating meaningful opportunities. Where outcomes are predetermined or preordained, people see less reason to participate, and so genuine choices, genuinely citizen-centered choices at the ballot box are the long-term answer.

We recognize in a challenging security situation there may be intermediate steps and there may be a path to be followed, but clearly, there has to be some hope for Egypt's young people that they will get back to the traditions that they have had of civil society being vibrant and citizen-centered government being the norm.

Mr. WILSON OF SOUTH CAROLINA. And again, I have seen it firsthand with IRI and NDI. Again, it is fun when you visit these countries and you can't tell who is R and who is D, which is amazing. But working together and by encouraging youth groups, different civic groups to participate, it is very positive, and I wish you continued success.

And I yield back to the chairperson.

Ms. ROS-LEHTINEN. Thank you so much, Mr. Wilson.

And now we will go to Mr. Trott, right? Yes.

Mr. TROTT. Thank you, Chairman, and——

Ms. ROS-LEHTINEN. Thank you so much.

Mr. TROTT [continuing]. I want to thank Ranking Member Deutch for scheduling this hearing.

And obviously, a discussion of the relationship between Egypt and the United States is very important because there is a strategic importance to the relationship.

I didn't get here in time to make an opening statement, but I wanted to mention to the panel that I am very honored today. I have a large Coptic community in my district, and so for the first time in the history of the House, Father Mina from the Orthodox church in Troy, Michigan, is here. He is going to open the House and lead the House in prayer later this morning——

Ms. ROS-LEHTINEN. Oh, terrific.

Mr. TROTT [continuing]. So it is a wonderful honor, and I will be happy to welcome him with the Speaker in about an hour.

My question goes to the events that happened a few weeks ago in Minya when the elderly woman was stripped naked and paraded around the city, and I just want each of the panelists to speak to, you know, what is going to be done in response to that outrageous incident? Is President Sisi going to be supportive of a rule-of-law solution? Are we going to engage in ridiculous reconciliation sessions? What is going to happen there? What can we do to help get the right result with respect to that outrageous behavior and incident?

And then generally with respect to religious minorities, how can Congress help move the needle to make sure the situation continues to improve particularly for the Copts in Egypt?

Ms. HAWTHORNE. I guess I will start with that one. First, in response to one of the earlier questions—and this actually feeds into your very important question with regard to how the U.S. can engage with Egypt on human rights and civil society and talk about the ways in which upholding these norms and values is in Egypt's interest—I would note that in recent meetings with visiting U.S. congressional delegations and with other foreign visitors, President Sisi has reportedly stated that the West should not hold Egypt to unfair Western human rights standards and that we should create sort of a lower standard or exceptions for Egypt's human rights performance.

But in fact it is very important to keep in mind that these standards are not Western standards. Many of them are enshrined in Egypt's new constitution of 2014. Egypt is also a signatory to several key international human rights instruments, and quasi-official human rights bodies in Egypt monitor human rights. So when President Sisi and other Egyptian officials make that assertion, I think we need to be ready to respond with the fact that these are really Egyptian norms and Egyptian demands, as well as universal ones.

With regard to the very troubling event that you referenced in Minya, frankly, this is one of the most disturbing things that I have read about of all the incredibly disturbing things that have been happening in Egypt recently. And sadly, it is a part of a pattern of communal tensions that lead to violent attacks on Coptic Christians with no recourse and no justice.

One of the disturbing elements of this incident was that it only came to light because of dogged local reporting and information on social media by Egyptian citizens. The Egyptian Government was originally prepared not to mention it.

President Sisi has spoken about this incident and has vowed that the perpetrators will be brought to justice, but I must say that under Sisi, under former President Morsi, and under former President Mubarak there was a terrible and disturbing pattern of lack of follow-through for these attacks against Copts and other minorities in Egypt, lots of nice words but very little follow-through or accountability or the rule of law.

The problem is is that the justice system, the judiciary in Egypt today, in many cases seems incapable of rendering justice, and there is an increasingly intolerant environment in Egyptian society against those who are different, which might include Copts and others who are part of the fabric of Egyptian society.

I think that it is very important that all visiting Americans—U.S. officials, Members of Congress, and others—raise these issues with President Sisi because the Egyptian authorities often would like to sweep these problems under the rug and suggest there is no sectarian tension and there is no communal strife in Egypt, and that is simply not the case. So the first step is for us to raise these issues and then to remind Egypt of its national and international obligations.

Mr. TROTT. Thank you. I think that is a great answer and a great suggestion and I appreciate it. And I have limited time, so I have just one other question I will follow up with you.

So if the Muslim Brotherhood have an exclusive ideology and democracy is an inclusive process, is the Muslim Brotherhood compatible with democracy?

Ms. HAWTHORNE. That is a crucial question and one that is difficult to answer in brief. I believe that at least through 2013 when President Morsi's government was toppled, there were members of the Muslim Brotherhood who were ready to work within and accept the democratic process while in my personal view still hewing to disturbing, illiberal, and intolerant views. But at least it was a first step that there were some members of the group who were willing to participate in elections and participate in a democratically elected government. However, once President Morsi was in power, we saw a lack of regard for human rights, norms, and many disturbing signs and tendencies toward repression.

However, if we look at actual acts and practices, we see that what has taken place under President Sisi, who professes to support democracy, is actually far more abusive and far more brutal and far more disparaging and violating of democratic norms than what took place under previous governments.

So I believe that there are many undemocratic actors in Egypt, not just many Islamists but also other Egyptians who are very enamored of a harsh, repressive security state. So the outcome on the ground is the same in my view, and it is very disturbing.

Mr. TROTT. Thank you. I yield back.

Ms. ROS-LEHTINEN. Thank you so much, excellent questions. And good luck with the prayer today.

Mr. Connolly of Virginia is recognized.

Mr. CONNOLLY. Thank you, Madam Chairman.

Ms. Hawthorne, your testimony is that the current crackdown is worse than that under Morsi and worse than that under the Mubarak government, correct?

Ms. HAWTHORNE. [Nonverbal response.]

Mr. CONNOLLY. That is a pretty hard statement. It seems to me that if you don't create political space, you are inviting repression and authoritarian regimes because there is no alternative. I don't know why we were surprised when Mubarak fell that the only viable electoral alternative was the Muslim Brotherhood. They were the only ones who had organized, however surreptitiously, and no other political dissent had been allowed, with our complicity. And we are doing it again under this military-led government.

And my friend from California, Mr. Rohrabacher, warned us that if we didn't support this government, the alternative was radical Islamic terrorism. I fear that without questioning this government, without challenging this government, without holding it to certain standards, that is precisely the alternative. We will create that alternative not by design, but because we have created no political space in Egypt, the largest Arab population in the world.

The idea that there is only this military-led government or chaos in the void seems to me an unacceptable proposition for the American people and the American Government, and we have to use whatever lever is available to us—and we have talked about that a little bit in terms of foreign assistance—to try to effectuate a better outcome and a better-performing government, one that is more inclusive and certainly does not resort—I mean, when you say, Ms. Hawthorne, that the current crackdown is worse than Morsi, whatever one wants to say about the Muslim Brotherhood government— and God knows I have no love for the Muslim Brotherhood government, but they did get elected freely and fairly according to the United States Government, is that not correct?

Ms. HAWTHORNE. [Nonverbal response.]

Mr. CONNOLLY. Did they mow thousands of Egyptian citizens in the streets of Cairo and Alexandria, Ms. Hawthorne?

Ms. HAWTHORNE. No, they did not.

Mr. CONNOLLY. No, they did not. That is kind of a big measuring stick, it seems to me. However repressive or anti-democratic tendencies they may have been showing at the time of the overthrow, they did not do what this government has done against its own citizens.

And I am not trying to create a favorable comparison, but I think we, America, we need to realistically look at what has been wrought in Egypt. And I believe that repressive government in Egypt plays into the hands of the very elements we want to oppose and we do not want to strengthen.

Ambassador Green, what about that? IRI is on the ground over there. You have had people who have been victimized by this government and the previous government. What is your sense?

Ambassador GREEN. Well, thank you, Congressman. If nothing else, your statement about the importance of political space we absolutely agree with, that there must be political space created for people to engage in a safe space with their government. And what we worry about is ongoing alienation of youth, the next generation. And if they grow up in a society with no safe space, no opportunities to engage with their government and with their society, what will be the long-term ramifications? Will you have an entire generation that knows nothing else but what they are seeing right now? And obviously none of us would support that. That would be a terrible thing.

53

Mr. CONNOLLY. And maybe that, given my limited time, Ambassador Green, we could talk just a little bit. I am going to invite you to describe the process. But when I met with the young people from the NGOs who are unfortunately being prosecuted by their government, these were young idealists committed to making their country a better place. I mean, you couldn't have asked for a better sense of citizenship. And in fact one worried about their idealism being perhaps crushed by the government. Most of them come from middle- and upper-middle-class families. They are educated. Describe the humiliation of what it means to be put on trial in a courtroom in Cairo. What happens? Are you put in a jury box?

Ambassador GREEN. They do not receive the same legal protections or opportunities obviously that we see in the United States or in nearly all of the civilized world. And it goes back to my strong belief that alienation of youth is one of the most dangerous conditions. Left unaddressed, it will guarantee more authoritarian government. It will guarantee an unsustainable security situation.

Mr. CONNOLLY. And the disillusionment of a cadre of young people who actually believed in democracy.

Ambassador GREEN. Very much so.

Mr. CONNOLLY. Thank you. Thank you, Mr. Chairman.

Mr. WILSON OF SOUTH CAROLINA [presiding]. And thank you, Mr. Connolly.

We will now proceed to Congressman Ron DeSantis of Florida.

Mr. DESANTIS. Thank you, Mr. Chairman. And I appreciate Chairman Ros-Lehtinen holding this hearing. I think that this is a very important subject.

And I agree with a lot of the concerns about what is going on in Egyptian society, but I also don't want to view the Muslim Brotherhood with any type of rose-colored glasses. I think that we should designate them as a foreign terrorist organization. We have passed it out of one House committee already, and it is awaiting Floor action. I think that they are not part of the solution in the Middle East but part of the problem.

So let me ask you, putting aside the problems that are going on in Egyptian society, Ambassador Green, is President el-Sisi a more reliable ally to the United States in combating Islamist terror than a Muslim Brotherhood-led government would be?

Ambassador GREEN. Thank you, Congressman. I am not sure I am qualified to comment necessarily on the security situation, but what I can comment on is very clearly former President Morsi and the Muslim Brotherhood were leading Egypt on a very, very dangerous path toward combative, violent Islamic extremism. You know, there is simply no doubt of that.

My fear and what my testimony is today is that in the 3 years since then, I worry that the clamping down on civil society and human rights is making the situation—we are certainly not improving the situation.

Mr. DESANTIS. I think we saw Mubarak is removed, they do an election, and really the default political movement is political Islam. You saw that with the Brotherhood winning; the Salafists did well in that election. And I am concerned as well with what you are talking about with civil society, but are there competing ideologies at play? Are there people who are trying to offer a more,

I think, appetizing view of the role of government and individual liberty in Egypt right now?

Ambassador GREEN. I think one of the dangers is when you have a total clampdown on civil society and the opportunities for citizens to engage their government, there is no pluralism, and that is a very dangerous thing. So, you know, it becomes a self-fulfilling prophecy. And again, we believe that there needs to be political space for people to express themselves. We recognize the security challenges that the government faces, but certainly from the perspective of the U.S., there is every reason that we should be clear-eyed in our analysis, and we should be honest and straightforward with those with whom we engage.

Mr. DESANTIS. Mr. Awad, what would you say? President el-Sisi, is he a more reliable ally in combating Islamist terror than a Brotherhood-led government would be?

Mr. AWAD. On that narrow question of reliability, to rely on a member of the Egyptian military over a member of the Muslim Brotherhood to combat terrorists, the short answer is yes. There was a question asked earlier about whether or not the Muslim Brotherhood is compatible with democracy. That question can be debated, but I believe they are wholly incompatible with liberal democracy. I am not really sure that this is a question that is necessarily up for debate, the Egyptian Muslim Brotherhood, that is.

On the question of whether or not they are a foreign terrorist organization, I don't necessarily see evidence that the entire organization is a terrorist organization. That does not make them pacifists. They have problematic views. They have proven themselves to be——

Mr. DESANTIS. They support groups like Hamas, though.

Mr. AWAD. They do support groups like Hamas. However, we are talking about material or financial support. The extent of that has to be investigated to be able to make a designation that every member of——

Mr. DESANTIS. Well, but they also provide——

Mr. AWAD [continuing]. The Muslim Brotherhood is a terrorist.

Mr. DESANTIS [continuing]. The intellectual contours for a really rigid political Islamism. And one of the things I appreciated with President el-Sisi—and again, I think I agree with you guys on the problems of the civil society is that he gave a speech in front of a lot of clerics in 2015 and just made the point that he is a devout Muslim, but you can't have the faith used to be antagonistic to every single person in the world who disagrees with that. I would imagine that that view would be rejected by the hierarchy of the Brotherhood, correct?

Mr. AWAD. That is true. And let me clarify. There is increasing evidence that one faction inside the Muslim Brotherhood has engaged in violence since January 2014 at least. Some of their members have engaged and do engage in violence. The question here is not, again, whether the Muslim Brotherhood is a pacifist organization or a problematic one. It is. It is incompatible with liberal democracy, and its views are regressive.

But for the United States in designating a foreign terrorist organization, if we want to take a step like that, perhaps we should take a look at the specific individuals or the specific faction that is actively engaging in these things because there are many members of the Muslim Brotherhood who may hold regressive views like members of white supremacist groups here in the United States that we wouldn't necessarily designate as terrorists. But again, the lack of designating as terrorists does not mean that the organization is a good organization or compatible with liberal democracy.

Mr. DESANTIS. All right. I thank the gentleman for his comments. I would just say I think that what is kind of at the foundation of society, are there pockets where you could actually have more liberal views about the proper role of government. And my fear is that the default is basically the Brotherhood and political Islamists, that that is where the majority or at least a plurality of the folks are. But I agree it is tough to figure that out if there are not open channels. But I appreciate the testimony, and I yield back.

Mr. WILSON OF SOUTH CAROLINA. Thank you, Congressman DeSantis. And now we will conclude with our guest, Congressman Dana Rohrabacher of California.

Mr. ROHRABACHER. Thank you very much, Mr. Chairman.

And I am very pleased to hear from our colleagues that we have a Coptic religious leader leading us in prayer this morning. That is a wonderful statement for us to make.

Let me suggest this. I worked in the White House with President Reagan at a time when the National Endowment for Democracy became real. I worked with a speechwriting team that developed the concept in his speech before Parliament. And let me note that during that time period, I think one of the reasons we won the cold war is Reagan became the champion of democracy rather than repression as a way to meet communism. That was part of the basic theory. But let me note this, that what we have today are alternatives between if the bad guys win, what we have is what, Islamic dictatorships that will murder people in great number.

And, you know, quite frankly, I think that when you have some level of repression against groups of people in your society that went to institute a dictatorship, what we did is we used those people who wanted freedom and democracy against a communist regime, we emphasized that, and that is how we won the cold war.

But the fact is those people and the institutes we are talking about were pushing for democracy in communist countries, and what would replace—in other words, the repressive people in those countries where the ones who didn't believe in democracy and we were supporting—by having the same strategy in Egypt and other countries, we are ending up, what, supporting and giving life to elements within that society that don't want more democracy.

So I would suggest that pushing against restrictions, especially during a time when hundreds of Egyptian people are being murdered or soldiers are being killed in a battle against radical Islam, at a time pushing them at that point to a standard, a Democratic standard that we believe should be the standard in ordinary times, perhaps makes it more likely that there will be a repressive government rather than less likely, meaning in the end I believe General Sisi, now President Sisi, wants a Democratic Egypt. And for us to undermine him now we might end up creating a horror story in terms of radical Islamic terrorism throughout the region, but also the people of Egypt will be less free if the Muslim Brotherhood element succeeds.

Now, with that suggestion, let me ask about the blasphemy law. You mentioned the blasphemy rules. How many people have been prosecuted for blasphemy laws in Egypt?

Ms. HAWTHORNE. I believe that in recent years it has been in the dozens.

Mr. ROHRABACHER. In recent years——

Ms. HAWTHORNE. Yes, it has been——

Mr. ROHRABACHER [continuing]. Been dozens?

Ms. HAWTHORNE [continuing]. In the dozens.

Mr. ROHRABACHER. So that means last year maybe one?

Ms. HAWTHORNE. No, I think it was a significantly more than that.

Mr. ROHRABACHER. Okay.

Ms. HAWTHORNE. I will have to check on those but——

Mr. ROHRABACHER. Five then——

Ms. HAWTHORNE [continuing]. I think it was——

Mr. ROHRABACHER. We are talking five or ten?

Ms. HAWTHORNE [continuing]. More than five, in the dozens.

Mr. ROHRABACHER. Okay. So in the dozens over a number of years. Tell me, in the other parts of the Middle East how does that stack up with the rest of the countries in the Middle East?

Ms. HAWTHORNE. Well, first of all, Egypt has a much larger Coptic Christian population——

Mr. ROHRABACHER. Yes.

Ms. HAWTHORNE [continuing]. Than many other countries.

Mr. ROHRABACHER. Right.

Ms. HAWTHORNE. So the dynamics are——

Mr. ROHRABACHER. That is because they have relative freedom of religion compared to all the other countries in the Middle East.

Ms. HAWTHORNE. I think it is very troubling. I mean, a recent incident that sort of highlighted some of the dilemmas that are occurring in Sisi's Egypt today is that a group of Coptic Christian teenagers who filmed——

Mr. ROHRABACHER. Hold on. Hold on. I am asking a question here. I don't want you to go on about your philosophy. We understand, and I agree with what you are saying, but I am asking you a specific question. Doesn't Egypt rank really high up on the scale when compared to other Middle Eastern countries in terms of freedom of religion, blasphemy, et cetera?

Ms. HAWTHORNE. In some respects there are positive signs. In other respects there are——

Mr. ROHRABACHER. Is the answer yes or no?

Ms. HAWTHORNE. I think it is a mixed picture.

Mr. ROHRABACHER. Okay.

Ms. HAWTHORNE. President Sisi has said some important things——

Mr. ROHRABACHER. All right.

Ms. HAWTHORNE [continuing]. But actions on the ground continue to be——

Mr. ROHRABACHER. All right. All right.

Ms. HAWTHORNE [continuing]. Increasingly intolerant.

Mr. ROHRABACHER. I have got a limited amount of time. That is why I can't let you go on. The bottom line is I have been to the Middle East, we have all been to the Middle East. To compare Egypt under attack by radical Islamic forces that hate us, that would murder us, as well as murder all the people in Egypt that disagree with them, to compare them to us and the rest of the Western world, Europe, is wrong. It is bad. It will result in more tyranny and not less. What is fair is to compare Egypt to the other Muslim countries in that region.

And I know it sounds like you are very hesitant to say it. I am not hesitant to say it. Egypt ranks way up there on the top of that scale. It is positive as compared to Qatar, as Saudi Arabia, Bahrain. All of these countries that we are talking about that you could compare it to legitimately, Egypt gets an A plus compared to them.

I think it is totally unfair, especially when this country is under attack, their people are being murdered, you have got the soldiers being killed, 900 soldiers—what would happen if 900 American soldiers—by the way, in proportion, that is about 90,000 American soldiers being killed and then to hold Egypt to that standard is wrong.

And, Mr. Chairman, just indulge me in one more moment. I do not believe that radical Islamic terrorists are really alienated Democrats. I don't believe that for a minute. This idea that because there have been clampdowns on certain people that maybe shouldn't be clamped down—look, any time you let the government bureaucracy go, they make mistakes and they target people. They do that—we have had our own people targeted here by our own Government in terms of the IRS, et cetera, for disagreement.

But this, the radical Islamists that are a threat to us now are not people who believed in democracy, but they were upset that they knew someone who was repressed by a repressive government. These are people who have a philosophy, an ideology like communism did during the cold war. The fact is that communists believed in what they believed in. They believed in a dictatorship of the proletariat. That idea was defeated, but we recognize what that was.

Today, radical Islamic terrorism is affecting the entire world and threatens especially the democratic world. General Sisi who is now President Sisi, the fact is if his government does not succeed because we have been too idealistic in comparing him to other standards, the Western standards of people who are not under attack and we lose this government to a radical Islamic government, the whole world will suffer and we will be in jeopardy.

With that said, thank you very much.

Mr. CONNOLLY. Mr. Chairman?

Mr. WILSON OF SOUTH CAROLINA. Yes, Congressman Connolly.

Mr. CONNOLLY. If I might be allowed just a brief response.

Mr. ROHRABACHER. That is a unanimous consent, but as long as you promise that someday I get that opportunity when you have refuted me.

Mr. CONNOLLY. Absolutely.

Mr. ROHRABACHER. Okay. Good.

Mr. CONNOLLY. I simply wanted to say that I don't know that we disagree. To be a critic of the el-Sisi government is not to view terrorists as lapsed Democrats. Some of us want to see, like you do, Mr. Rohrabacher, Egypt as a bulwark against terrorism and extremism. The question is how best to do that. And some of us respectfully, including the witnesses here today, believe that the path el-Sisi has gone down actually will not yield that result, will do the opposite, not by design but by practice.

Now, maybe we are wrong and I hope we are, but it is worthy of examination because my friend and I share the same goal. It is a question of how best to get there. I don't believe the best way to get there is by killing your own citizens, by clamping down on civil liberties, by imprisoning and trying young idealist NGO staffers who are trying to make for a better Egypt. I believe that those actions are almost designed to play into the hands of the very people you and I want to prevent from coming to power.

And that is the debate. It is not an either/or choice of do you like terrorists or do you want a military strongman who cracks down on all dissent. There has to be another alternative making this better, creating political space so that we aren't faced with a black-and-white, either/or alternative. And that is just my point of view. Thank you, friend.

Mr. WILSON OF SOUTH CAROLINA. And I would like to thank, as we conclude, Congressman Rohrabacher and Congressman Connolly for their input, and we appreciate so much the witnesses here today.

And again, I just have to restate IRI, NDI, the National Endowment for Democracy, what a difference it makes around the world providing opportunity. And I just wish the success of each of you.

We are now adjourned.

[Whereupon, at 11:25 a.m., the subcommittee was adjourned.]

APPENDIX

Material Submitted for the Record

SUBCOMMITTEE HEARING NOTICE
COMMITTEE ON FOREIGN AFFAIRS
U.S. HOUSE OF REPRESENTATIVES
WASHINGTON, DC 20515-6128

Subcommittee on the Middle East and North Africa
Ileana Ros-Lehtinen (R-FL), Chairman

June 8, 2016

TO: MEMBERS OF THE COMMITTEE ON FOREIGN AFFAIRS

You are respectfully requested to attend an OPEN hearing of the Committee on Foreign Affairs, to be held by the Subcommittee on the Middle East and North Africa in Room 2172 of the Rayburn House Office Building (and available live on the Committee website at http://www.ForeignAffairs.house.gov):

DATE: Wednesday, June 15, 2016

TIME: 10:00 a.m.

SUBJECT: Egypt: Challenges and Opportunities for U.S. Policy

WITNESSES: The Honorable Mark Green
                   President
                   International Republican Institute

                   Mr. Mokhtar Awad
                   Research Fellow
                   Program on Extremism
                   Center for Cyber and Homeland Security
                   George Washington University

                   Ms. Amy Hawthorne
                   Deputy Director for Research
                   Project on Middle East Democracy

By Direction of the Chairman

The Committee on Foreign Affairs seeks to make its facilities accessible to persons with disabilities. If you are in need of special accommodations, please call 202/225-5021 at least four business days in advance of the event, whenever practicable. Questions with regard to special accommodations in general (including availability of Committee materials in alternative formats and assistive listening devices) may be directed to the Committee.

COMMITTEE ON FOREIGN AFFAIRS

MINUTES OF SUBCOMMITTEE ON _____*the Middle East and North Africa*_____ HEARING

Day___*Wednesday*___Date_____*June 15, 2016*_____Room_____*2172*_____

Starting Time _____*10:01*_____Ending Time _____*11:25*_____

Recesses |____| (____to ____) (____to ____) (____to ____) (____to ____) (____to ____) (____to ____)

Presiding Member(s)

Chairman Ros-Lehtinen, Rep. Wilson

Check all of the following that apply:

Open Session ☑   Electronically Recorded (taped) ☑
Executive (closed) Session ☐   Stenographic Record ☑
Televised ☑

TITLE OF HEARING:

Egypt: Challenges and Opportunities for U.S. Policy

SUBCOMMITTEE MEMBERS PRESENT:

Chairman Ros-Lehtinen, Reps. Chabot, Wilson, DeSantis, Yoho, Trott, and Zeldin
Ranking Member Deutch, Reps. Connolly, Frankel, and Cicilline

---

NON-SUBCOMMITTEE MEMBERS PRESENT: *(Mark with an * if they are not members of full committee.)*

Rep. Rohrabacher

HEARING WITNESSES: Same as meeting notice attached? Yes ☑ No ☐
(If "no", please list below and include title, agency, department, or organization.)

STATEMENTS FOR THE RECORD: *(List any statements submitted for the record.)*

Rep. Cicilline

TIME SCHEDULED TO RECONVENE _____
or
TIME ADJOURNED _____*11:25*_____

Subcommittee Staff Director

David N. Cicilline
Foreign Affairs MENA Subcommittee
"Egypt: Challenges and Opportunities for U.S. Policy"
June 15, 2016

Thank you Chairwoman Ros-Lehtinen and Ranking Member Deutch for calling this hearing on Egypt. Thank you to the witnesses for being here today. I look forward to hearing your testimony.

Egypt is at an important point in its post-Mubarak, post-Morsi transition. So far, the Al-Sisi government has placed a premium on security over democracy or civil rights. With parliamentary elections having been completed late last year, it is critical that the United States push the Sisi government to respect the rule of law and move toward a system that protects the rights of its citizens and recognizes separation of powers.

Our policies toward Egypt should reflect not just the important security relationship, but also the reality that the model of supporting an autocratic regime is inherently unstable in the long-term. We must push the Al-Sisi regime to enact democratic reforms and respect fundamental human rights, or Egypt may find itself, once again, in turmoil.

U.S. policy towards Egypt over the past few decades had some significant flaws. We propped up an unpopular, repressive dictator who abused his people at the expense of his political cronies, and watched on the sidelines as the Egyptian people finally rose up against this repressive system. I am concerned that we are very quickly forgetting the past and are poised to repeat history for the sake of stability.